D1262419

Algrove Publishing Limited
1090 Morrison Drive
Ottawa, Ontario
Canada K2H 1C2

**Canadian Cataloguing in Publication Data**

Main entry under title:

Decorative carving, pyrography and Flemish carving

(Classic reprint series)
Reprint, with original title pages, of Wood-carving for day schools, recreative evening classes and the home / by G.C. Hewitt. Halifax : F. King & Sons, 1900, and, Pyrography and Flemish carving / by T. Vernette Morse. Chicago : Art Craft Institute, 1903.
ISBN 1-894572-03-3

1. Wood-carving. 2. Pyrography. I. Hewitt, G. C. Woodcarving for day schools, recreative evening classes and the home. II. Morse, T. Vernette, b. 1852. Pyrography and Flemish carving. III. Series: Classic reprint series (Ottawa, Ont.)

TT180.D42 2000 736'.4 C00-900781-4

Printed in Canada
#10800

# *Publisher's Note*

It is always a risk to combine two titles when reprinting. In the current case, there is much more material on woodcarving than there is on pyrography, but the two books were so complementary that it seemed a shame not to tuck a second book inside the binding, given the nominal additional cost of the extra few dozen pages and the substantial extra cost of binding them separately.

Should the reader feel mislead, we will accept all reasonable criticism and accede to any reasonable demands for retribution.

Leonard G. Lee, Publisher
Ottawa
July, 2000

# WOOD-CARVING

FOR

DAY SCHOOLS,

RECREATIVE EVENING CLASSES

AND THE HOME.

BY

G. C. HEWITT,

*Author of "Constructive Teaching," "Carton Work," &c.*
*Diplomê of the German Manual Training Association, and of the Karlstadt (Sweden) Sloyd Seminarium.*
*Examiner of Wood-carving to the "Educational Handwork Union."*

HALIFAX:
F. KING & SONS, LTD., PRINTERS, PUBLISHERS, SCHOOL OUTFITTERS, &c.

1900.

# CHAPTER I.

In looking through the Reports of the Government Inspectors on Evening Continuation Schools one is particularly struck with the large number of unsuccessful classes. Here and there a statement is made of a district containing good classes, where the interest has been maintained to the end of the session, but in many cases a great falling off towards the end of the term is the most striking characteristic. In many cases they have failed through want of being more practicable. Only in rare cases are the schools "Continuation Schools" in a real sense. A boy at the day school has been taught a little geometry and drawing, but he has never been able to make practical use of his learning in that direction. In places where manual training has been taken in evening classes he now sees how the principles may be applied. There are, however, many places where wood-work cannot be taken either from want of suitable premises or from the cost of apparatus.

The next best course to fall back upon is wood-carving, which can be carried on in the School without the use of benches, and with but few tools. Where manual work has been taken up, it has invariably been successful. Mr. Legard, says: "Manual work, for example, is always attractive, particularly if it is accompanied by drawing." Mr. Cowie, says: "Drawing is frequently taught, and wood-carving continues to be popular." Mr. King, says: "In Somerset, wood-carving seems to be the favourite subject." Mr. Wilson, says: "I have again to speak highly of the spirited and successful manner in which the Halifax Recreative Continuation Schools are conducted." In these classes manual work is taken. In an article by Mr. J. E. Flower, M.A., on Evening Recreative Classes he strongly recommends that all young scholars should be encouraged, as far as possible, to take Drawing and Design and some kind of Hand-work, such as modelling or carving.

The course of carving contained in this handbook is based on geometrical drawing. If carving is taken in an evening class it is most essential that the student should spend part of the time at geometry.

Mr. Ablett, Director of the Drawing Society of Great Britain and Ireland, says: "Chip-carving provides an exercise as interesting to youth as whittling a stick. There can be no dispute as to its practical value in training the hand to deftly use a simple tool, and in showing the artistic effects which may be obtained in the employment of geometrical drawing—that universal language of the workman." Another writer says: "I cannot speak too strongly of my belief in the value of geometrical drawing or the charm it has for the pupils. The neat little instruments, the care they need, the well sharpened pencils and the delicacy and neatness needed in the construction of the figures, are quite an education in themselves; and the symmetry of the figures made with them is the best possible training for eye and hand." Chip-carving is a very old method of decorating wood. Early specimens of this style of decoration are found in many museums, both in England and on the continent. In Norway, Sweden, Germany, and Switzerland, it is still extensively practised at the present day. The course contained in this book is largely based on the German and Swedish system. It may be worked by anyone who has patience and is neat in the use of compass and ruler. The work does not require any great manual effort, and is undoubtedly of a fascinating nature. The greater part of the designs may be worked with two tools, viz.: a bevelling chisel (A) and a veining chisel (B); a holdfast (c)

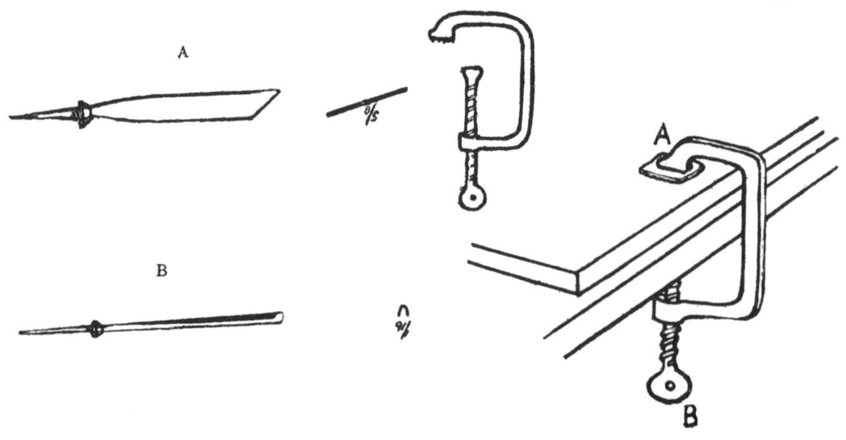

would also be required to fix the wood to the desk. The cost of these three tools is very small, and the pupil will, in most cases, willingly purchase them. When the design is worked from the black-board, it is an advantage to use coloured chalks to show the shading. It is also a good plan to work the designs a fairly good size, and upon no account whatever to use dark coloured woods.

The woods most commonly selected are alder, lime or maple; though pear. oak, walnut, or mahogany may be used. For sides of blotting books and other outside decorations, thick linoleum may be used. It is particularly easy to cut, and is very effective.

In most of the earlier examples it will be noticed that the part to be taken out is triangular in shape. The first cut is from A to B, and is made by the bevelling chisel (Fig. 1); the deepest part of the cut being at the point A; the second part of the cut is from A to C. The triangle, A B C, is then taken out with the same tool (Fig. 2). In design No. 2, a small triangle is taken out with the veining chisel.

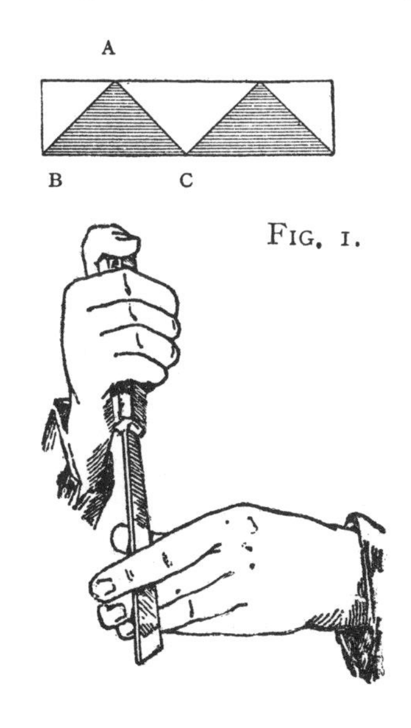

Fig. 1.

Fig. 2.

## DESIGN No. 1.

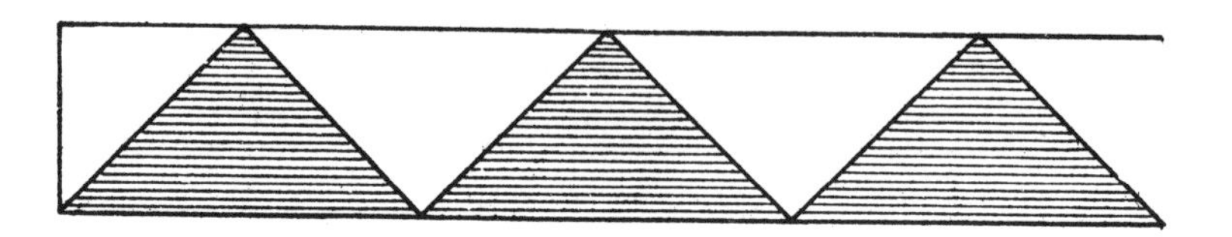

## DESIGN No. 2.

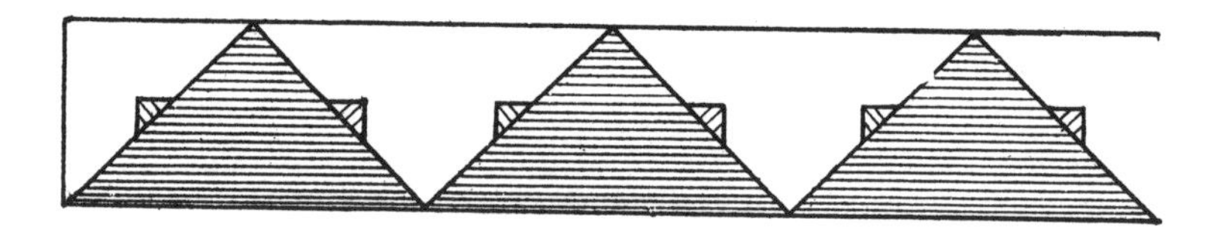

## DESIGN No. 3.

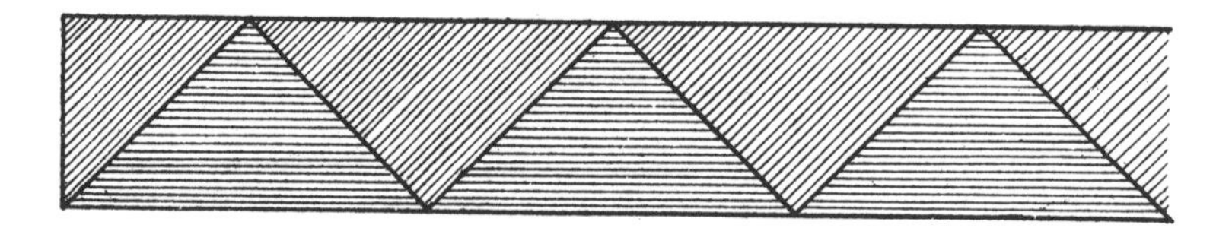

## DESIGN No. 4.

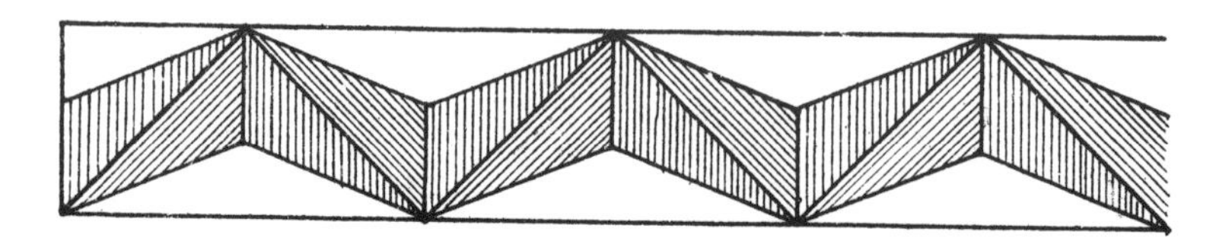

## DESIGN No. 5.

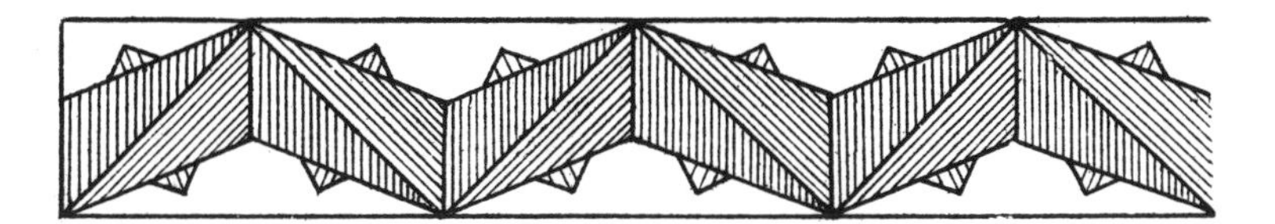

## DESIGN No. 6.

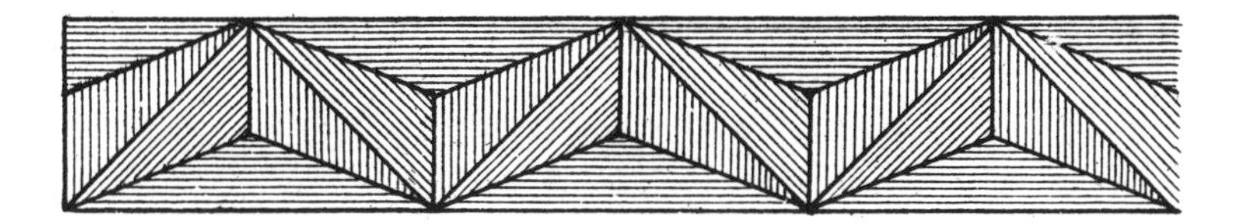

## DESIGN No. 7.

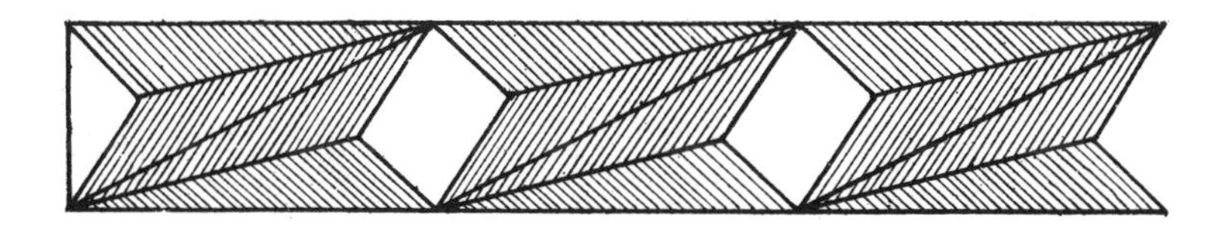

## DESIGN No. 8.

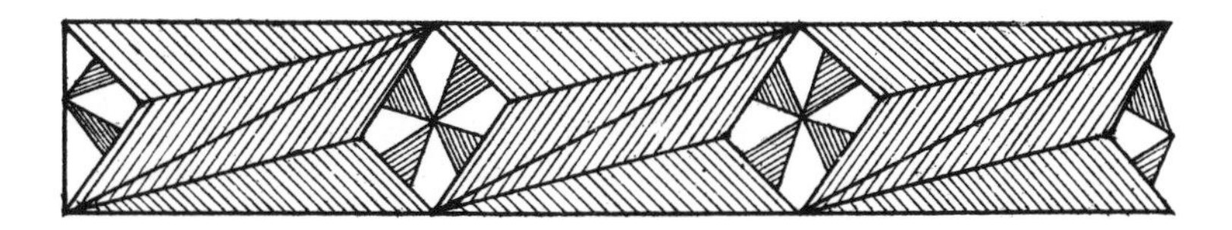

## DESIGN No. 9.

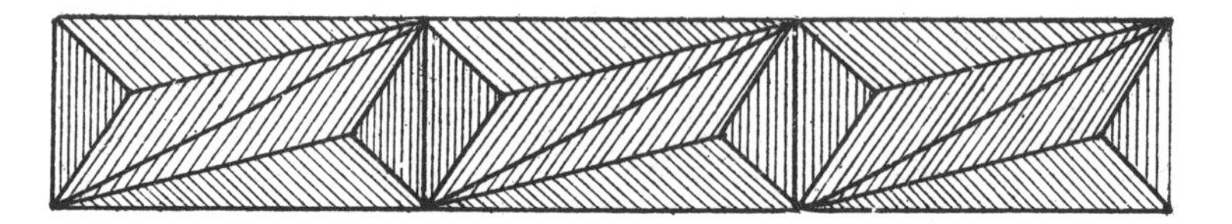

## DESIGN No. 10.

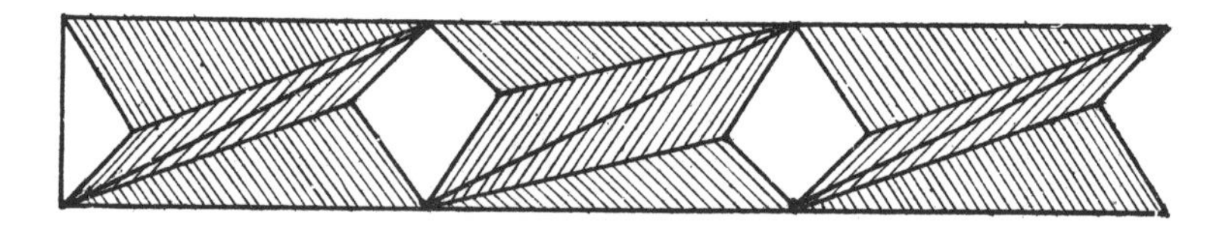

## DESIGN No. 11.

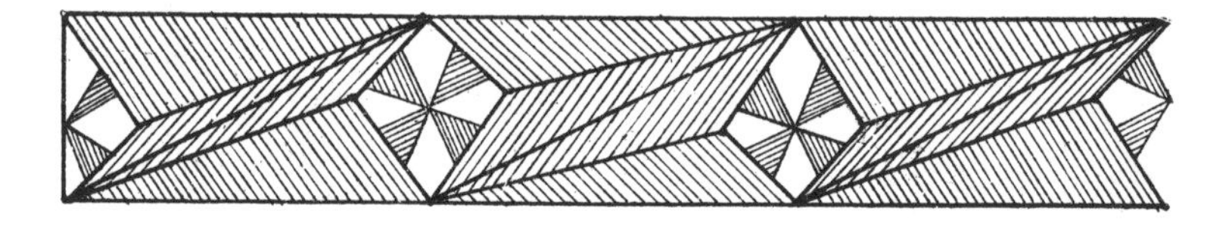

## DESIGN No. 12.

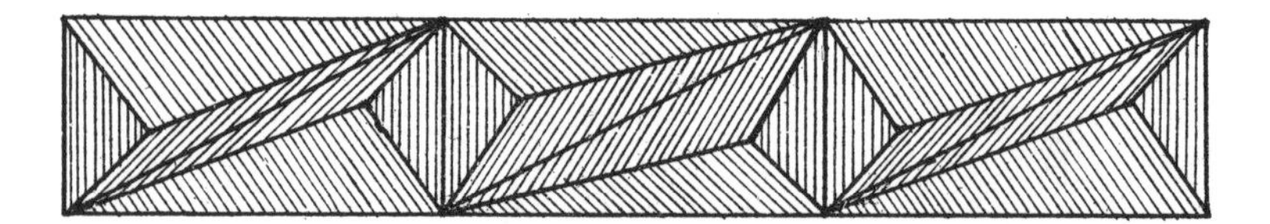

### DESIGN No. 13.

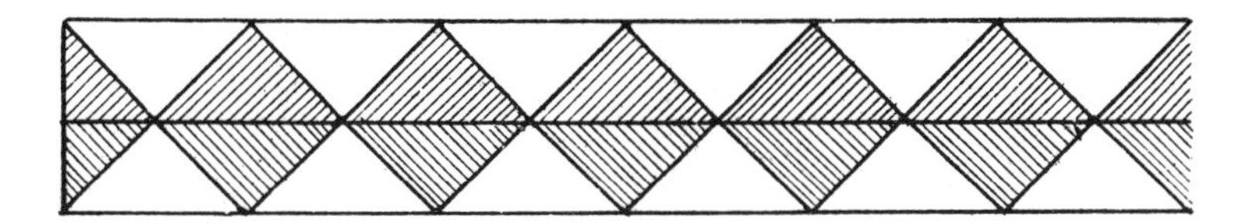

### DESIGN No. 14.

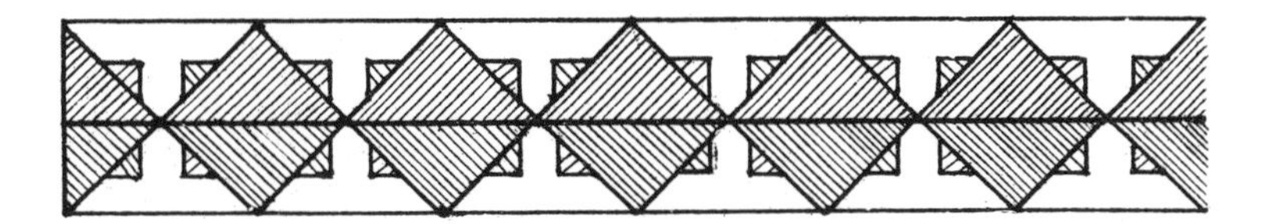

### DESIGN No. 15.

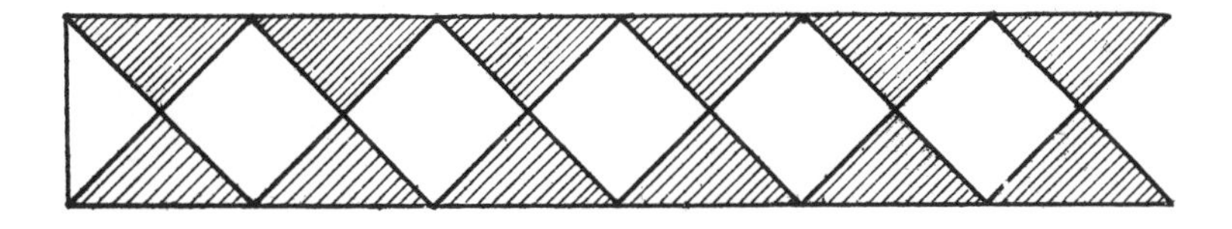

### DESIGN No. 16.

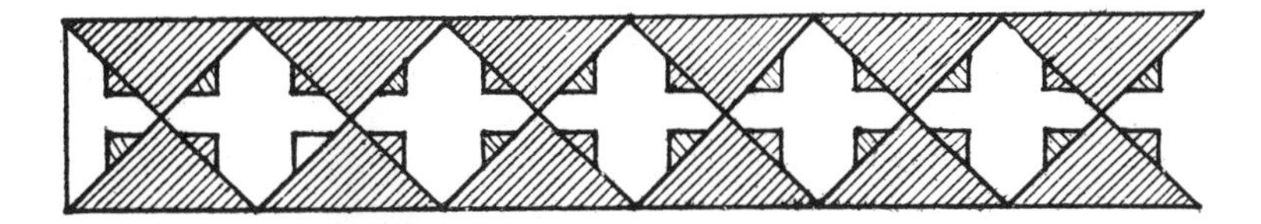

## DESIGN No. 17.

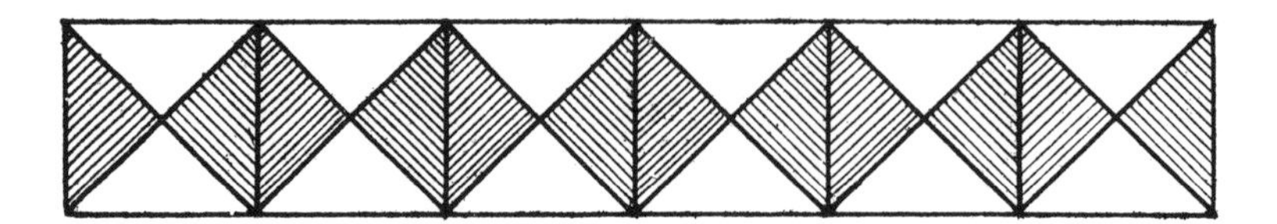

## DESIGN No. 18.

## DESIGN No. 19.

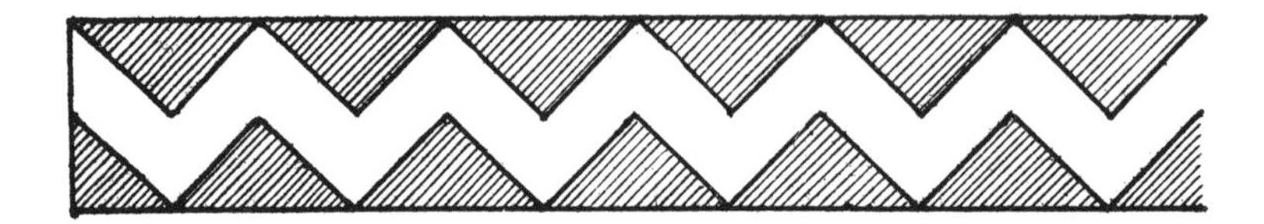

## DESIGN No. 20.

## DESIGN No. 21.

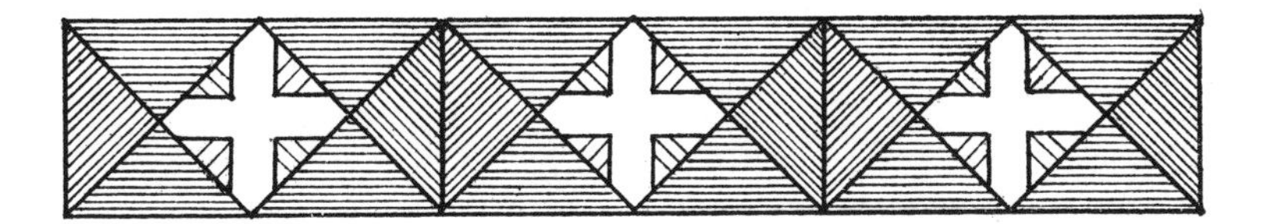

## DESIGN No. 22.

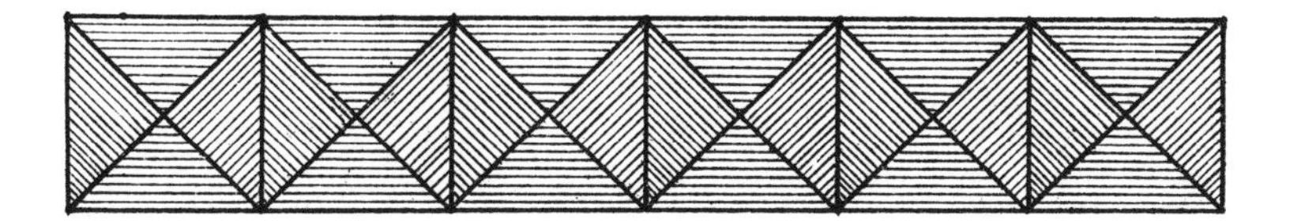

## DESIGN No. 23.

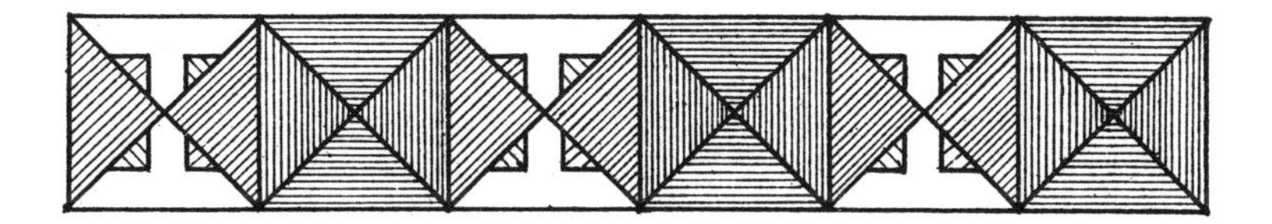

## DESIGN No. 24.

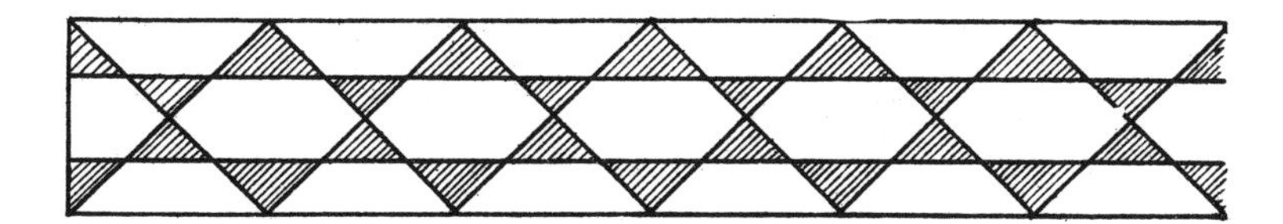

## DESIGN No. 25.

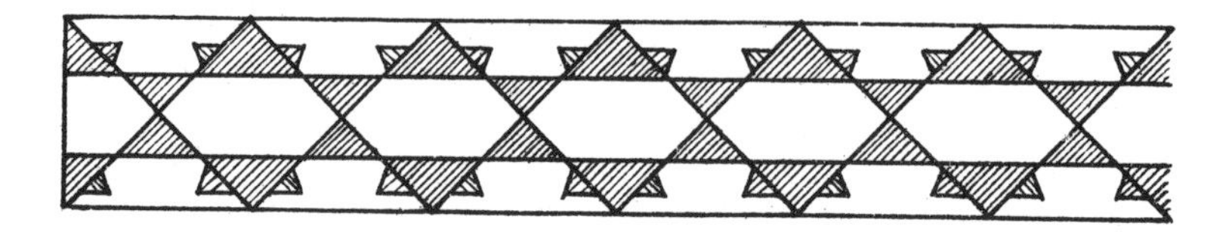

## DESIGN No. 26.

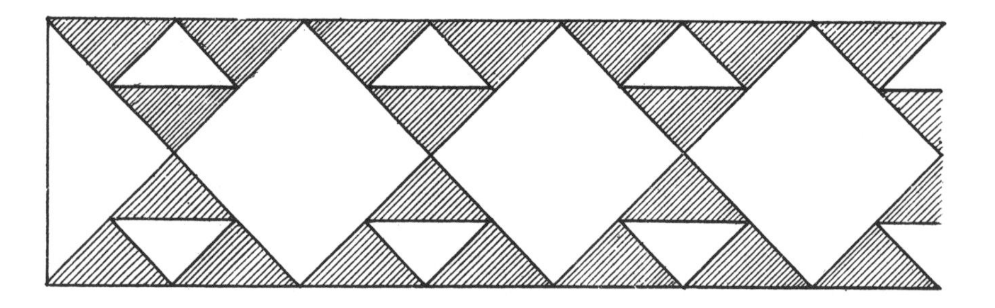

## DESIGN No. 27.

## DESIGN No. 28.

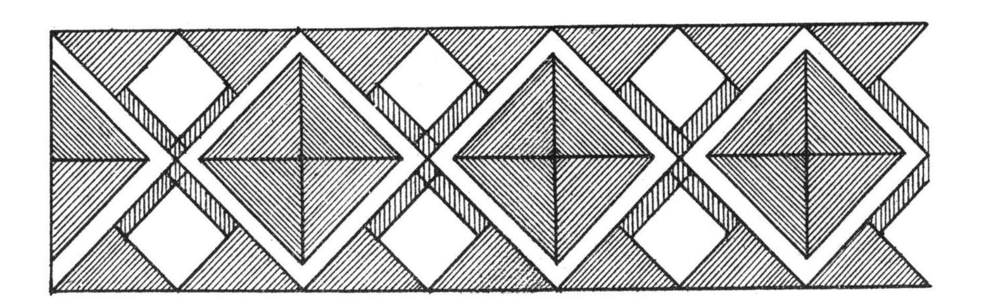

## DESIGN No. 29.

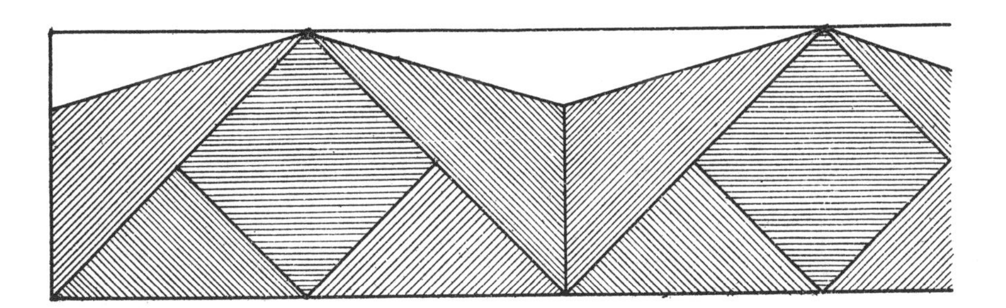

## DESIGN No. 30.

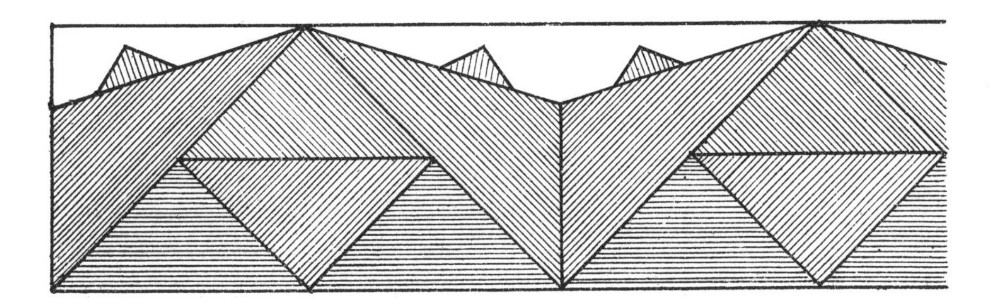

## DESIGN No. 31.

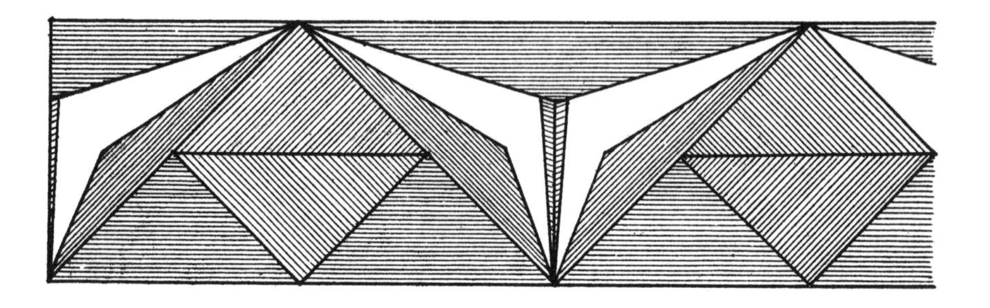

## DESIGN No. 32.

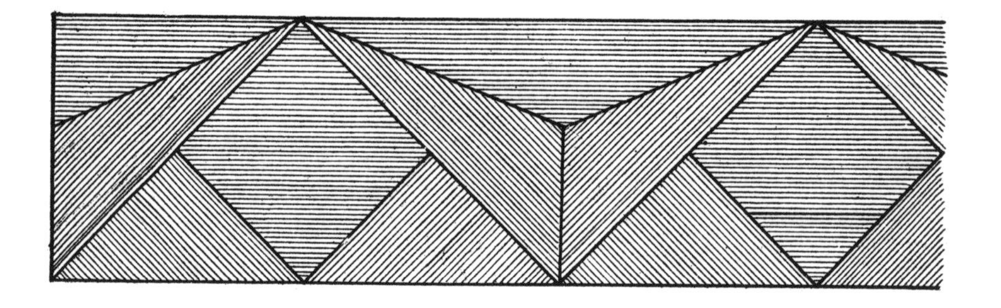

# CHAPTER II.

ALL the designs from 1 to 32 were straight cuts. In No. 33 will be found the first curved cut. If the design is examined it will be seen that the parts to be taken out are still triangular with one curved side. The same chisel may be used, but more care will be required with the curve. The advantages of the curved cuts over the straight, are that more freedom is given to the hand, and the student is prepared for relief carving.

The exercises from 37 to 44 require particular care in maintaining a good line from points A′ to B′.

The dotted ground, shown in No. 55, is made by a punch, for which an ordinary French nail blunted at the point may be used. Hold the nail with the thumb and finger, resting the wrist on the wood, and gently tap with a light mallet. If required, punches may be obtained from the publishers, and used in place of the nail. Their use is to mark or decorate the ground, in order to "throw up" or contrast it with the ornament.

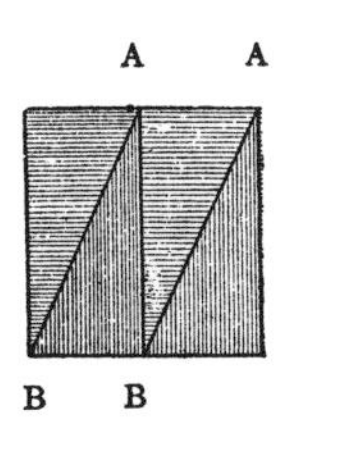


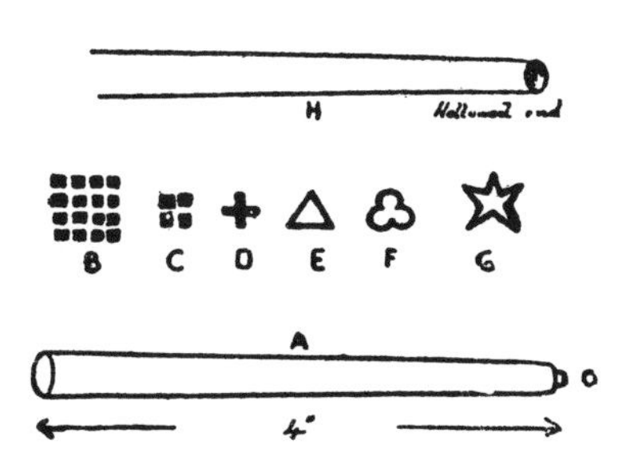

## DESIGN No. 33.

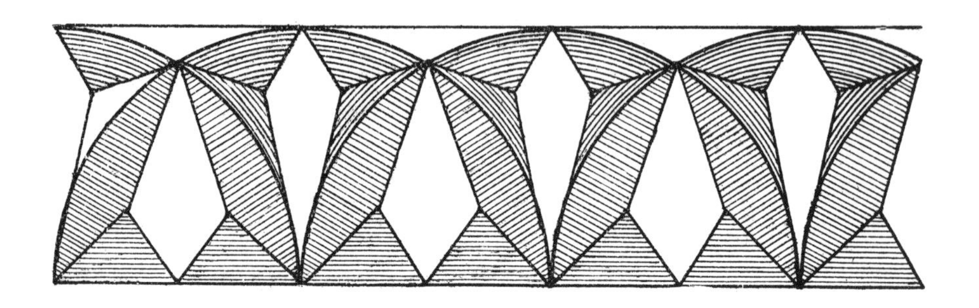

## DESIGN No. 34.

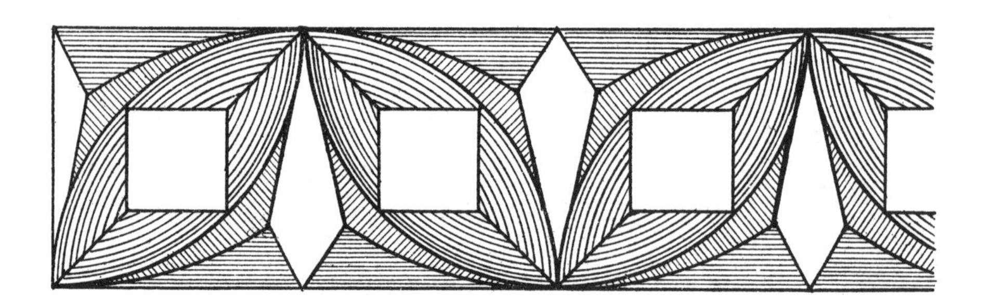

## DESIGN No. 35.

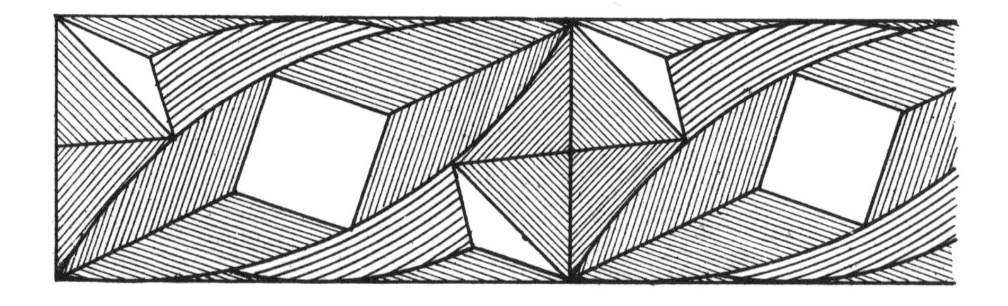

## DESIGN No. 36.

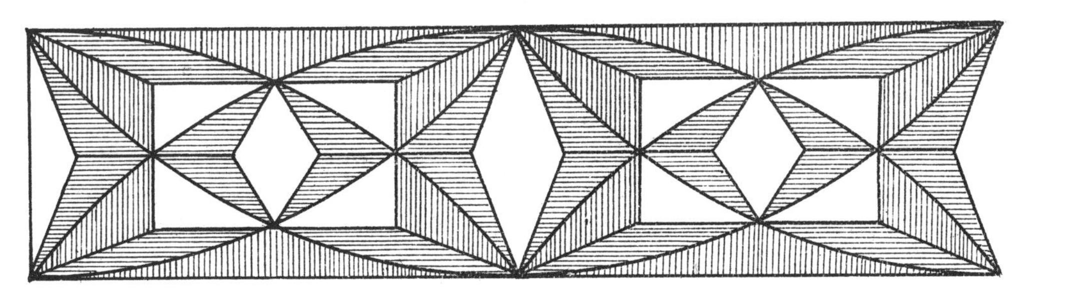

## DESIGN No. 37.

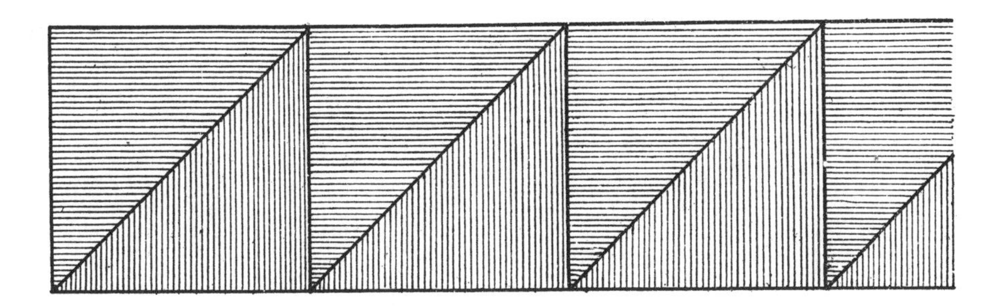

## DESIGN No. 38.

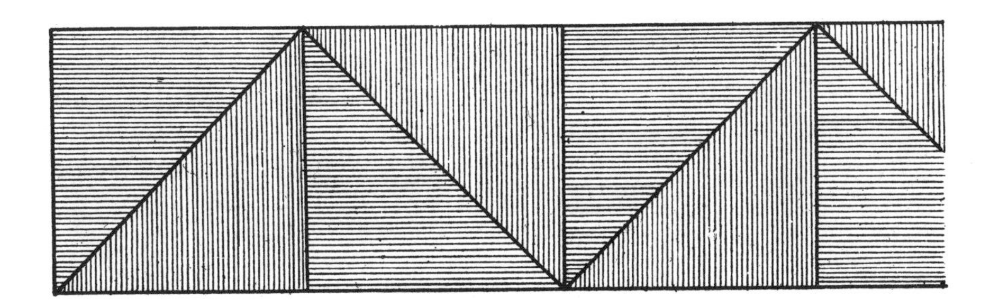

## DESIGN No. 39.

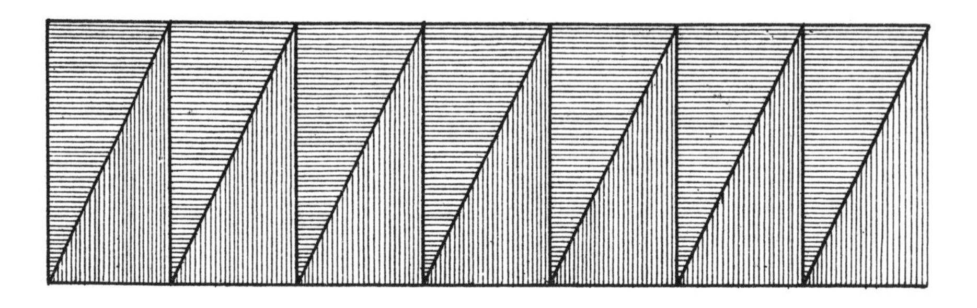

## DESIGN No. 40.

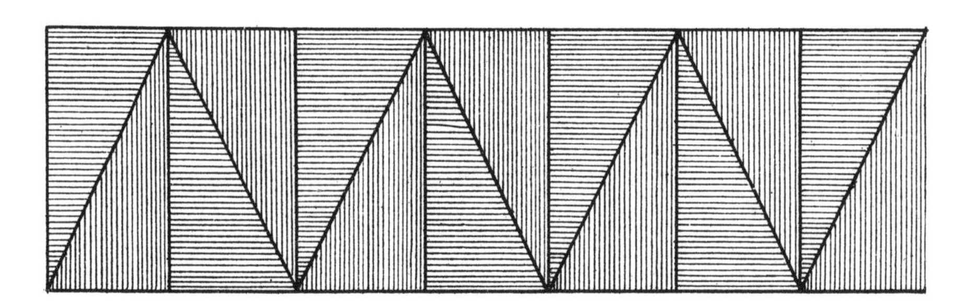

## DESIGN No. 41.

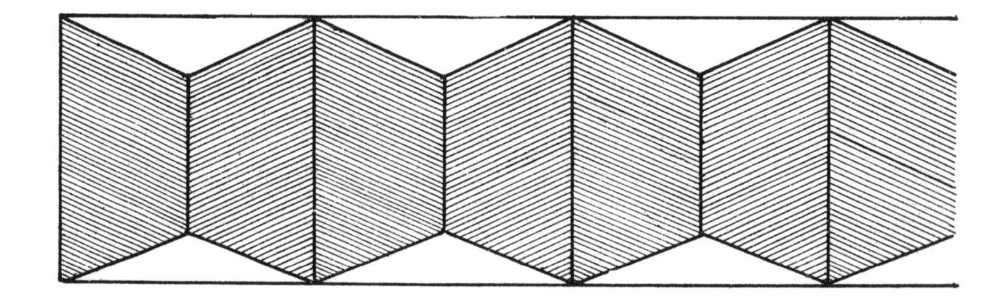

## DESIGN No. 42.

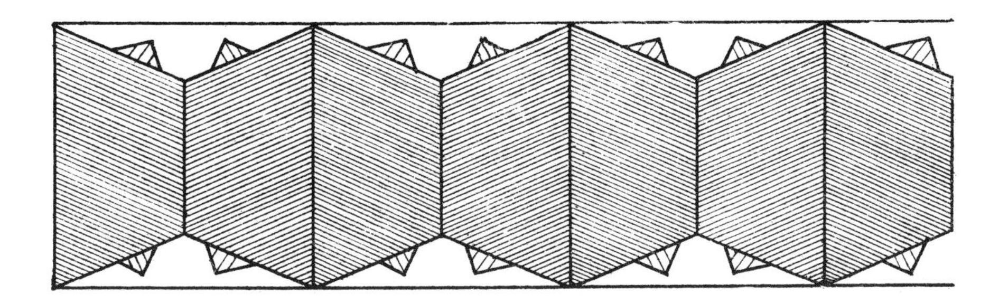

## DESIGN No. 43.

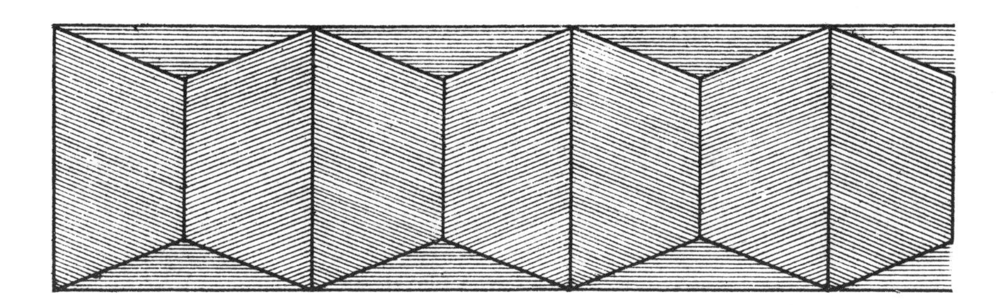

## DESIGN No. 44.

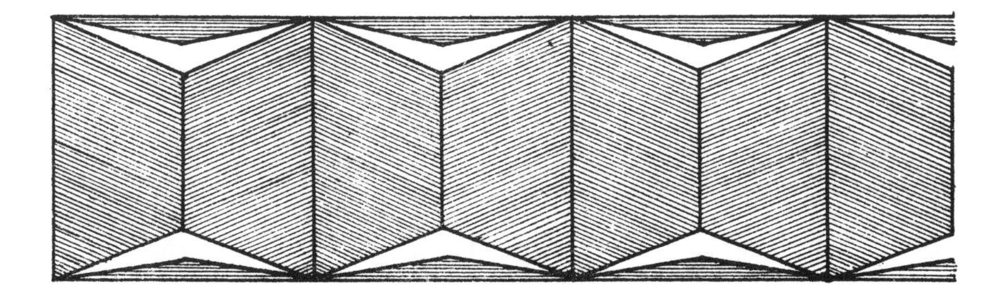

## DESIGN No. 45.

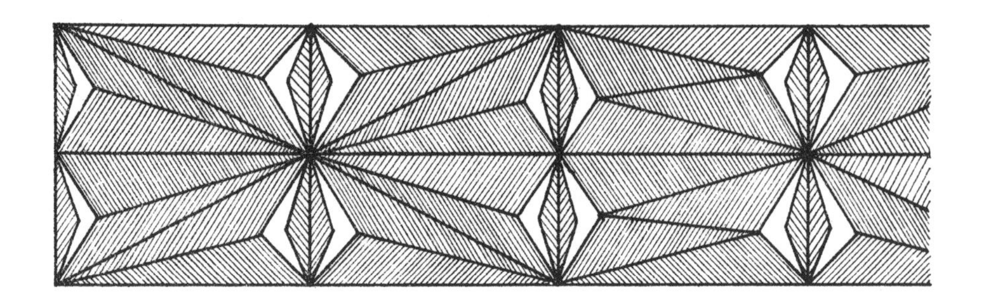

## DESIGN No. 46.

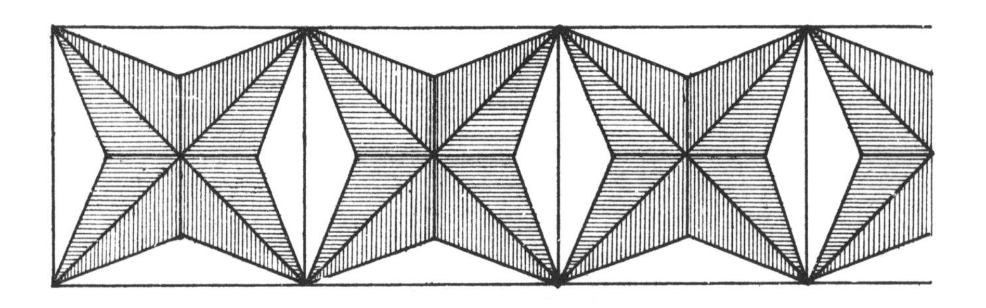

## DESIGN No. 47.

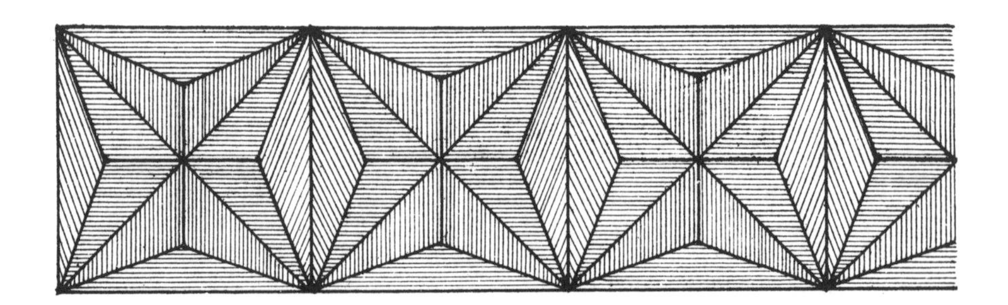

## DESIGN No. 48.

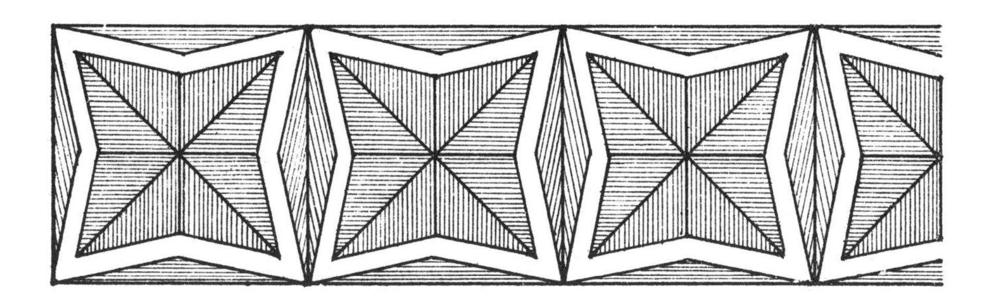

## DESIGN No. 49.

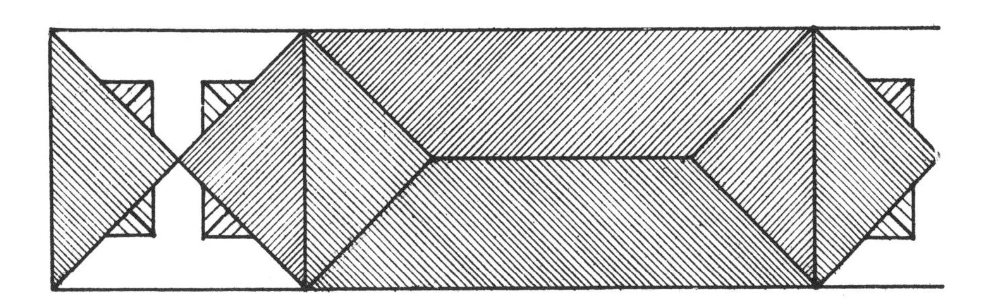

## DESIGN No. 50.

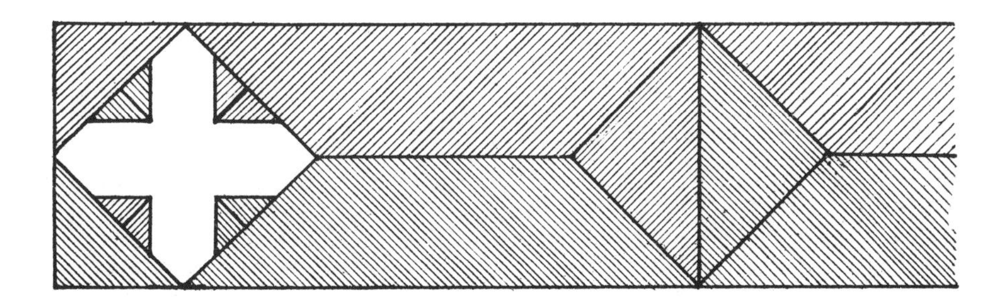

## DESIGN No. 51.

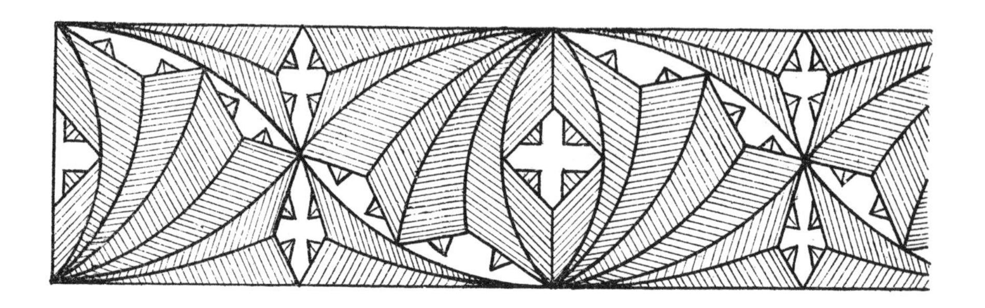

## DESIGN No. 52.

## DESIGN No. 53.

## DESIGN No. 54.

## DESIGN No. 55.

## CHAPTER III.

In some of the following designs the firmer chisel and the gouge could be used with advantage, viz.:—in No. 62. The firmer would be of use in the cut

The gouge will be of use in some of the curved designs.

No. 56. Design for inkstand. Hole in the centre for glass ink well. Place a small block of wood on each of the four corners to form legs.

No. 57. Design for a ruler or picture frame, using the alternate designs, A, B.

No. 58. Picture frame: may be made of lime or maple.

No. 59. Handle of paper knife: may be made of maple or other hard wood.

No. 60. Do.

No. 61. Centre.

No. 62. Side of book stand. Two of these will be required. They should be fixed to A——B the piece A, B, by hinges.

No. 63. Picture frame: may be made of walnut or mahogany.

No. 64. A centre.

No. 65. Side of blotter, card case, or side of book: pear.

Nos. 66 & 67. Centres.

No. 68. Back of small bracket. Shelf and support placed in the position of the dotted lines.

## DESIGN No. 56.

## DESIGN No. 57a.

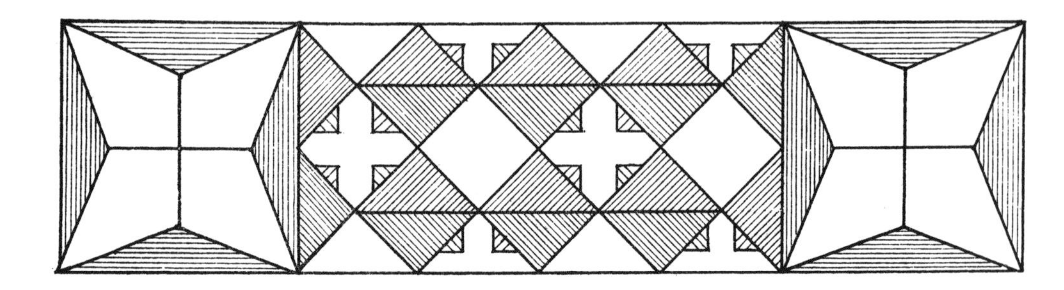

## DESIGN No. 57b.

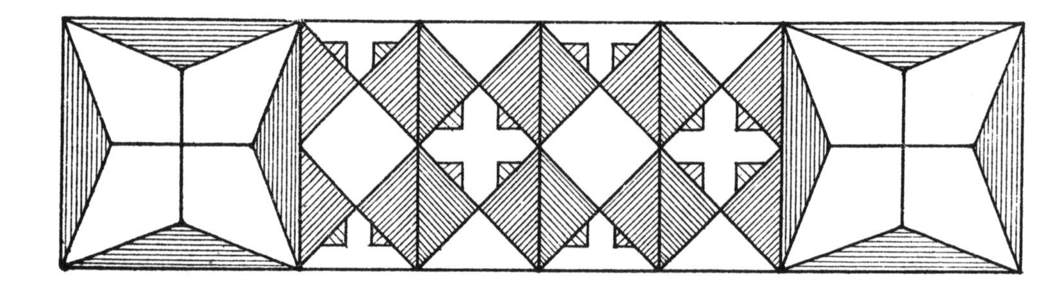

## DESIGN No. 58.

DESIGN No. 60.

DESIGN No. 59.

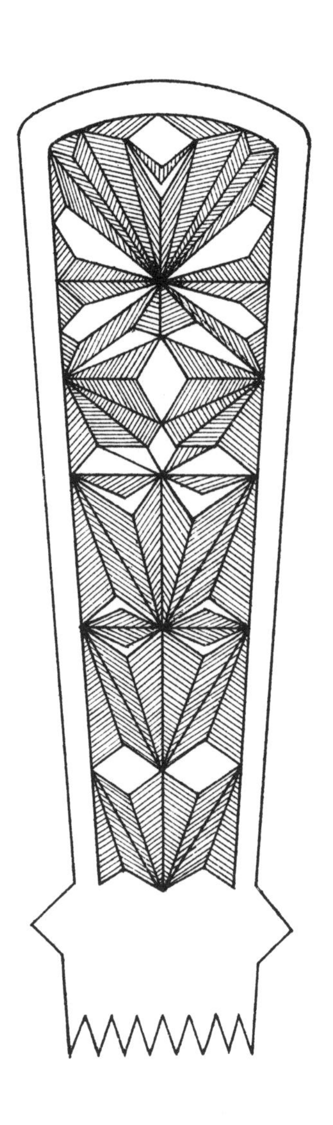

## DESIGN No. 61.

## DESIGN No. 62.

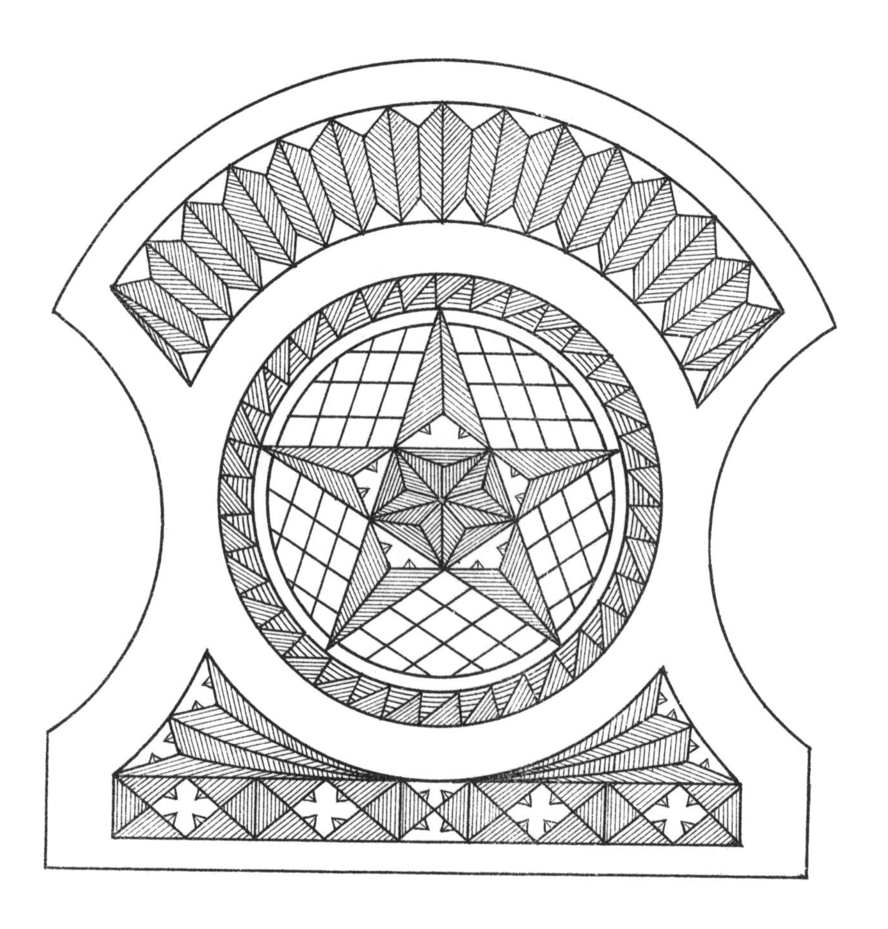

## DESIGN No. 63.

## DESIGN No. 64.

## DESIGN No. 65.

## DESIGN No. 66.

## DESIGN No. 67.

**DESIGN No. 68.**

# CHAPTER IV.

Up to the present but little use has been made of the veining chisel. Its chief use is to take out little V shaped pieces in most of the designs from 2 to 25. In the examples I to XV., at the end of this chapter, are a number of exercises in the use of this tool. The lines in the examples may be drawn on the wood, and then cut out with the veiner. Place the tool at the commencement of the line on the right hand side, with the hollow part uppermost. Let the right hand grasp the tool by the end of the handle and place the left in front of the right; the latter will guide the tool along the line to cut it out, while the former will prevent it from slipping. The veining chisel is used for edging patterns, and is much used in Sweden for the "Old Peasants' Style" of carving. In the exercises XII. to XV. practice is given in curves, and a number of very pretty designs may be made. Great care will be required to make the furrow the same depth and width.

DESIGN No. I.

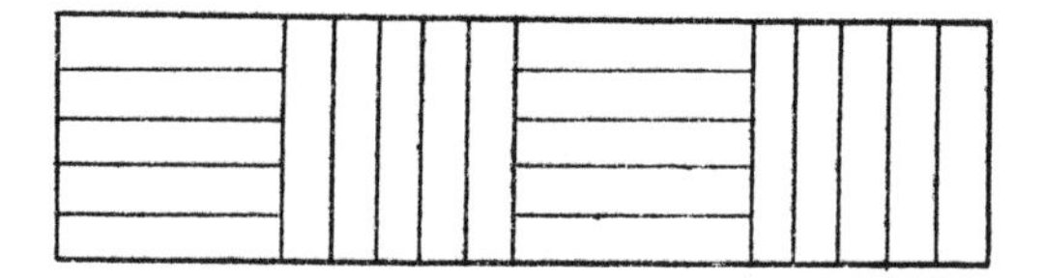

DESIGN No. VII.

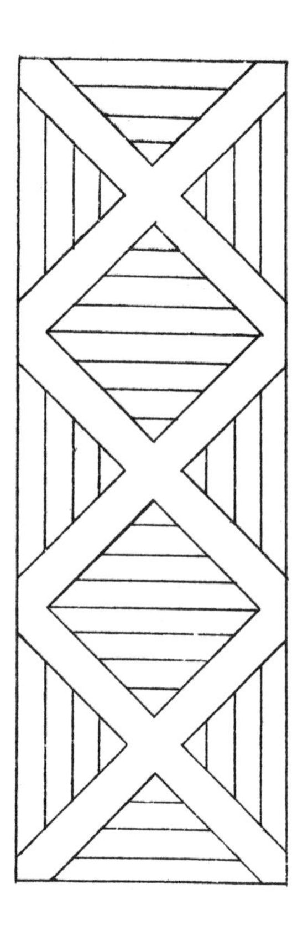

DESIGN No. II.

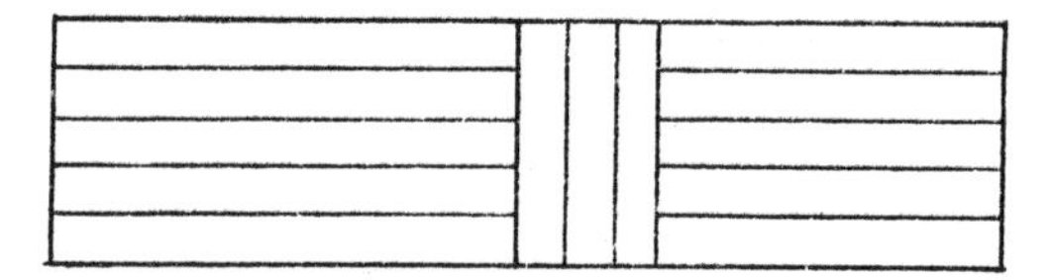

DESIGN No. III.

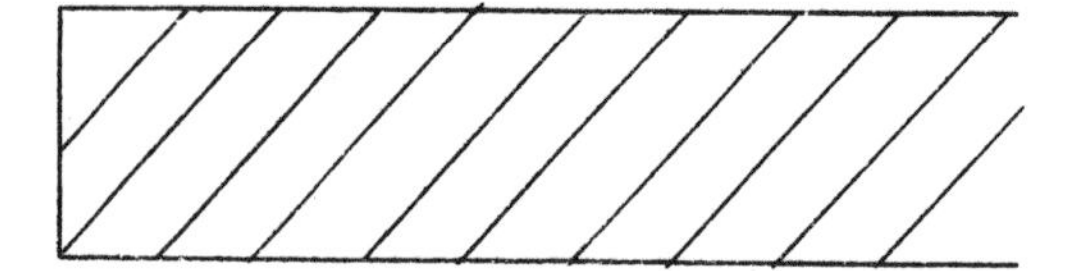

DESIGN No. IV.

DESIGN No. V.

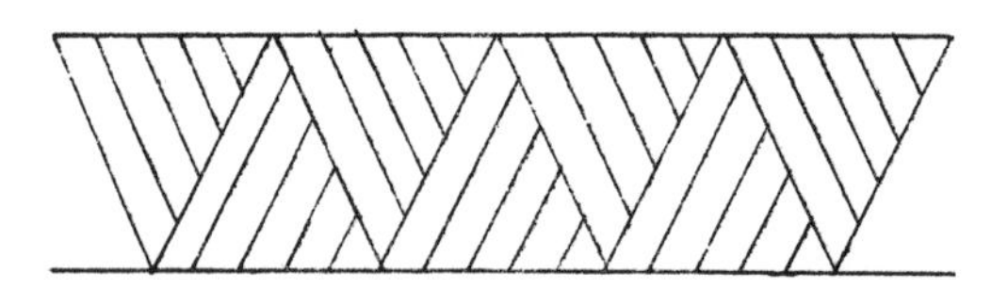

DESIGN No. VI.

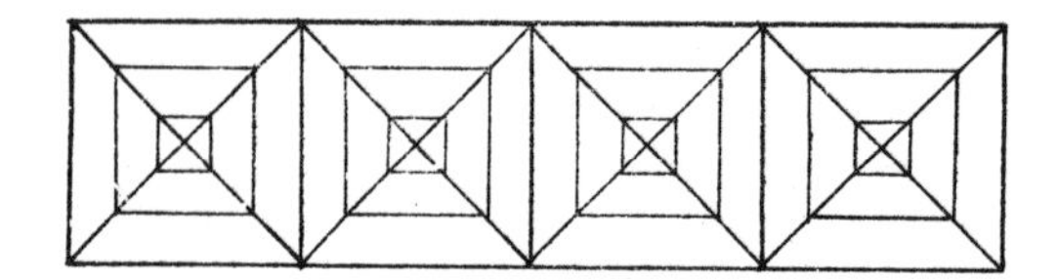

## DESIGN No. VIII.

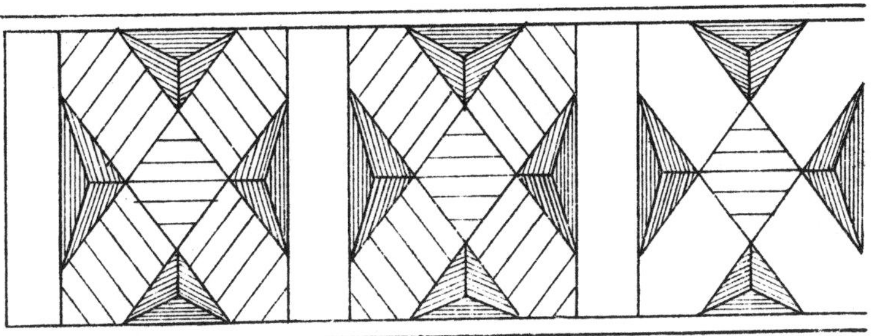

## DESIGN No. IX.

## DESIGN No. X.

## DESIGN No. XI.

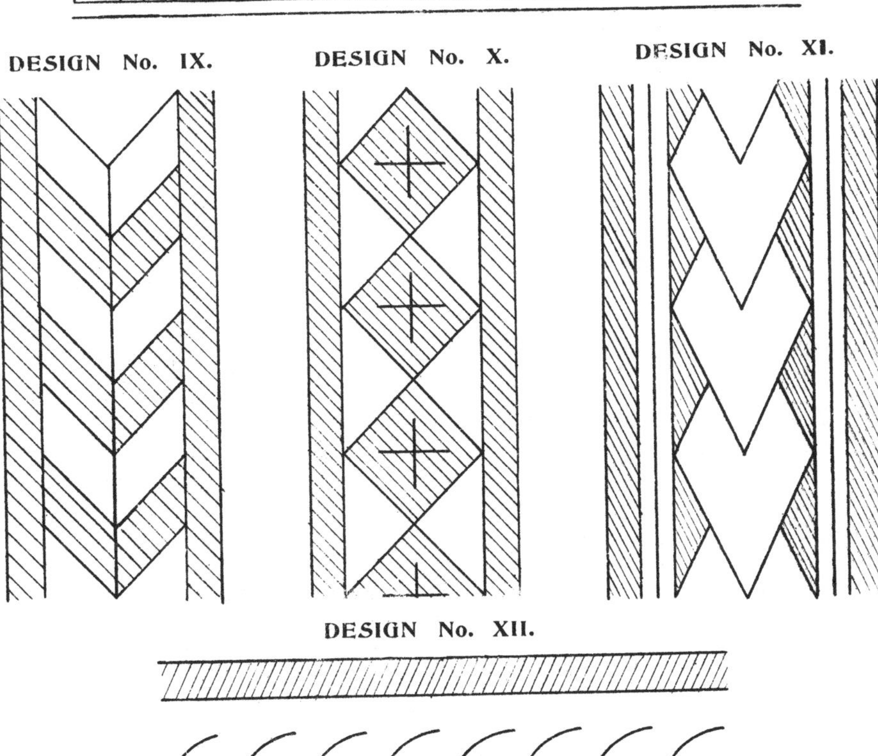

## DESIGN No. XII.

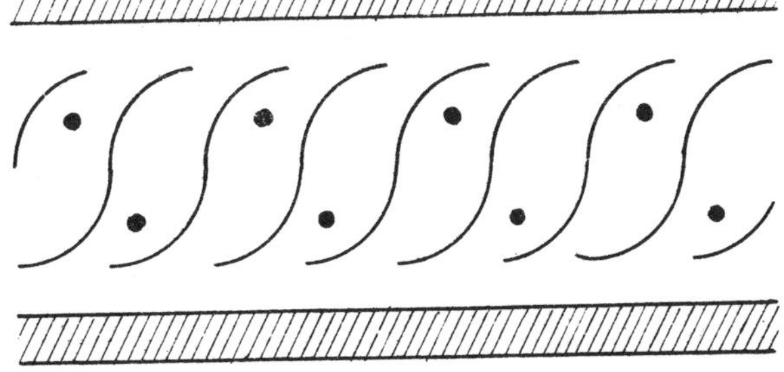

## DESIGN No. XIII.

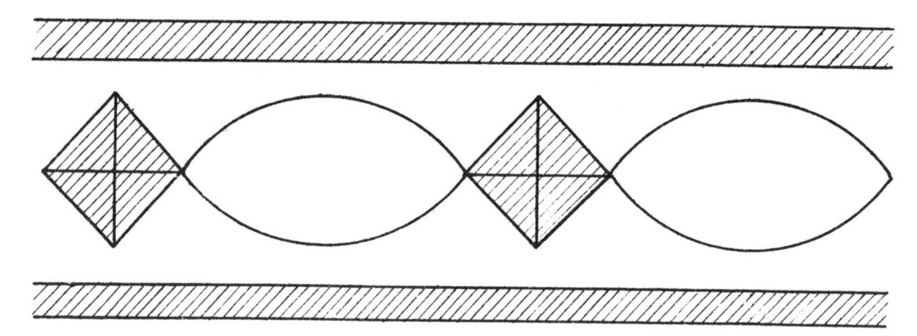

## DESIGN No. XIV.

## DESIGN No. XV.

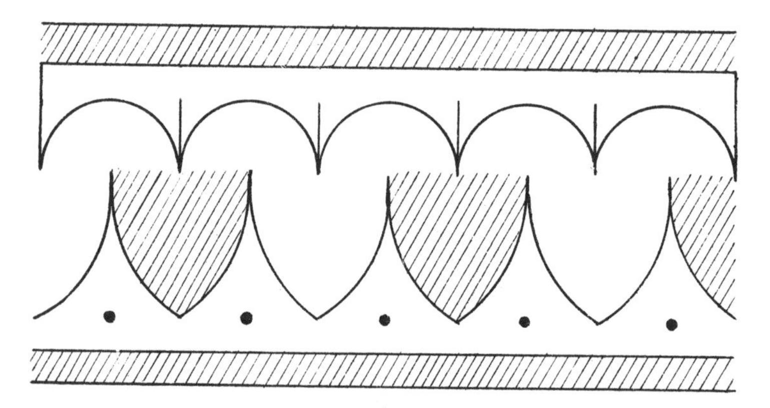

# CHAPTER V.

The designs from 69 to 81 are specimens of the "Old Peasants' Style" of wood-carving found so plentifully in Scandinavia.

Nos. 69 and 70 are designs for handles of paper knives. They are each in very low relief: the design having been cut round first by the veining tool. The ground is then taken out and punched as shown.

No. 71 is a design for a ruler or the end of a small box. There is no grounding out in this, the design being cut round with the veiner.

No. 72 is a design for a card case or the side of a small book, and may be made of pear.

No. 73. Lid of box. Design cut round with a veining tool, and the ground worked up with a punch.

No. 74. A ruler or picture frame.

No. 75. Card case.

No. 76. Centre for panel. Design cut round with veiner.

Nos. 77 & 78. Card cases or sides of book.

No. 79. Lid of box. The illustration shows only half of the design.

No. 80. Centre for lid of box and part of the border.

No. 81. Portfolio cover. The illustration shows only one quarter of the design. The two borders cut out with the bevelling chisel. The centre design traced round with the veiner.

DESIGN No. 69.

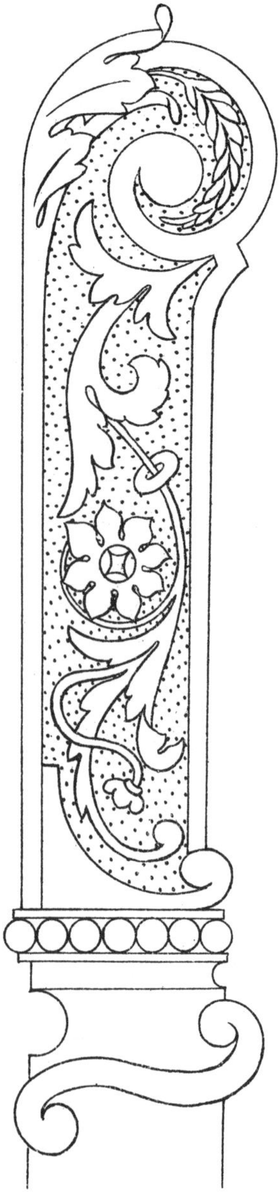

DESIGN No. 70.

DESIGN No. 71.

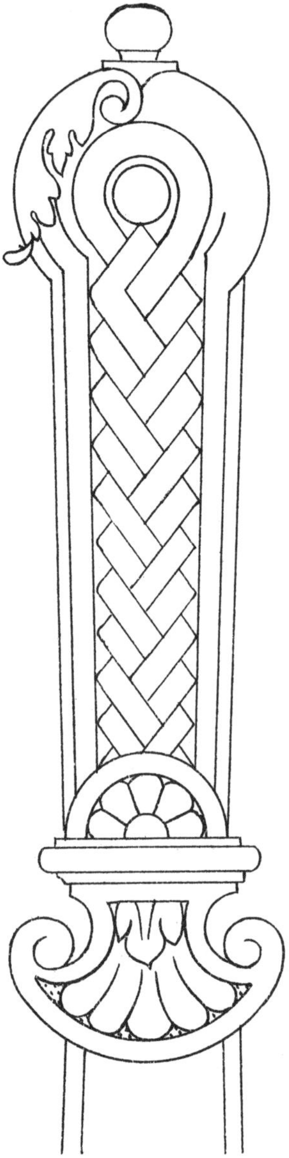

**DESIGN No. 72.**

**DESIGN No. 75.**

DESIGN No. 73.

DESIGN No. 74.

## DESIGN No. 76.

## DESIGN No. 77.

## DESIGN No. 78.

**DESIGN No. 79.**

## DESIGN No. 80.

## DESIGN No. 81.

## CHAPTER VI.

In some cases it is expedient to cover the wood with some proctecting substance. It is not a good plan to varnish the model; it destroys the finish of the cuts and gives a common place appearance. A good composition for coating a model is made of bees' wax and turpentine. The mixture is spread over the object with a fine brush. After the model has been left a short time to dry, brush with a stiff brush until a faint polish appears. If the student wishes to go further into the matter of staining, varnishing, and polishing, I would recommend him to obtain a little book published by Cassell's, entitled, "Wood Finishing."

# PYROGRAPHY
# and
# FLEMISH CARVING

BEING THE SECOND BOOK OF THE

# HOW TO DO IT

SERIES

BY

T. VERNETTE MORSE

Author of Art Study Courses and Basket Making.

**Illustrated with nearly One Hundred Working Designs.**

CHICAGO.

ART CRAFT INSTITUTE

1903.

# PREFACE.

In issuing the second edition of Pyrography and Flemish Carving, the author is pleased to express a feeling of gratification for the many appreciative letters that are daily received from students and teachers who are finding this series of books helpful in their work. It is quite impossible to put into book form the actual teachings in any department of a school, especially when the work is thoroughly practical in every respect.

Books, as teachers, may lack the individuality of the instructor, and the equipment of the school but they are ripe in suggestions, and consequently occupy an important place in educational work.

Replying to the question, as to the work of the Art Craft Institute, the writer takes this opportunity to state that it is a series of shops, founded on the principles of drawing, designing and modeling. Students are taught, not only to draw and design, but to make the finished article from their own designs. That article may be a chair for the home, a piece of silver for the table, a gown for the street, or it may be purely decorative like embroidery and other fine needlework.

Pyrography, like all other decorative work, has its place and some beautiful pieces have been made at the school, Many of these are illustrated in this work with directions for making, with the hope that they may assist those who wish to study this facinating art without the aid of a teacher.

Letters containing two cent stamp will be cheerfully answered.

*T. Vernette Morse.*

# CONTENTS.

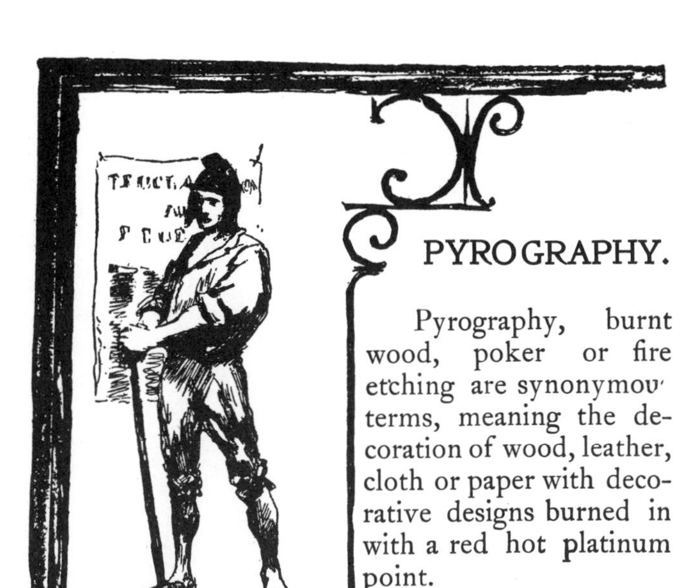

## PYROGRAPHY.

Pyrography, burnt wood, poker or fire etching are synonymous terms, meaning the decoration of wood, leather, cloth or paper with decorative designs burned in with a red hot platinum point.

It is not, as many may suppose, a new art, but a revival of the times when there was no dividing line between the fine and applied arts.

Such great men as Cellini practiced carving in connection with poker etching and color, and some fine specimens are attributed to his skill.

In Germany, Holland and Prussia, there are many Inns which still bear traces of poker decorations, executed bv artists who lived a hundred or more years ago.

Even in New York state, there is an old tavern with a door decorated in this style. The story is, that it was done by a queer old dutchman, who visited the tavern some time in the fifties, remaining long enough to paint a portrait of the landlords charming young daughter. As portraits were rare at that time, to own one was considered a mark of high distinction, and this portrait painted by the Flemish artist, who spent his evenings doing poker and smoke etchings to amuse the crowd, is now one of the cherished possessions of a well known society woman of New York, who is fortunate in being the grandaughter of the original. But the decorations of the door have been scrubbed, and scoured by a succession of immaculate housekeepers until but little of their former unique character remains.

Pyrography in those days, was done by heating a poker red hot in the fire or forge, today, thanks to the fertile mind of some inventor, we have the perfectly adjusted platinum point as easily managed as a pencil or pen.

Any one who can draw can do the work perfectly, and for those who can not draw there are many useful articles already stamped with reliable patterns that are beautiful when finished in simple outline.

To the artist who can paint and draw there are but few suggestions to make; to others we would say, learn to draw and design if you wish to do really beautiful work that will stand the test of time.

Pyrography as a decoration has come to stay. Like all other things that are new, novel and apparently easy, it will have to pass through a certain "fad stage" before reaching a recognized position, of worth, but never the less the artist who takes it up seriously, recognizing its possibilites and keeping within them, may go on from year to year adding to the importance of the art.

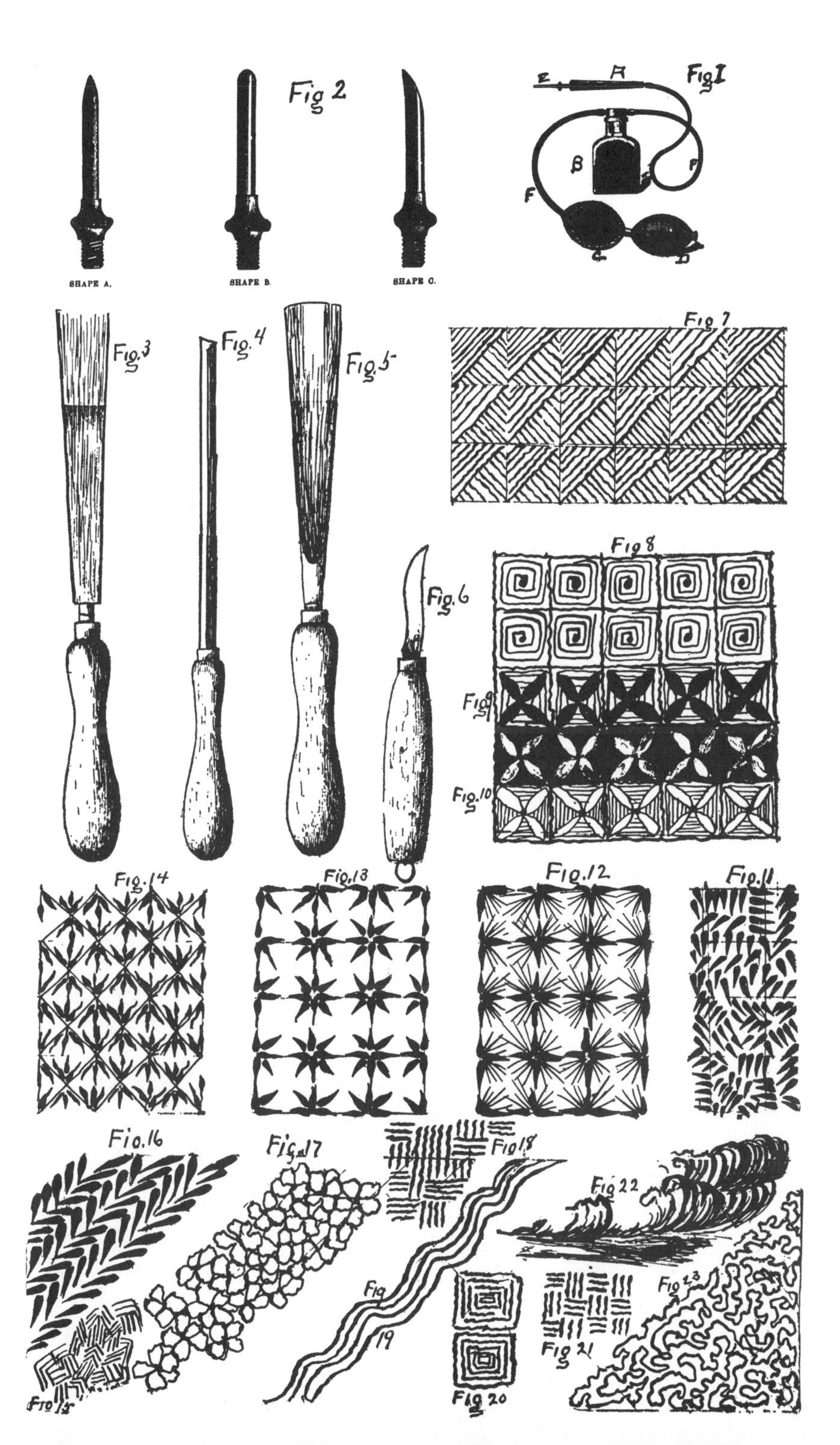
Fig 2
Fig I
SHAPE A.
SHAPE B.
SHAPE C.
Fig. 3
Fig. 4
Fig. 5
Fig 7
Fig. 6
Fig 8
Fig 9
Fig. 10
Fig. 14
Fig. 13
Fig. 12
Fig. 11
Fig. 16
Fig. 17
Fig 18
Fig 22
Fig 19
Fig 23
Fig 21
Fig 20
Fig 15

An entire outfit (see Fig. 1) may be purchased for, from four to six dollars, we do not recommend the cheaper ones.

Considerable practice is required to acquire dexterity with the point. It is difficult, at first, to work with freedom, as one hand is occupied in working the bulb to keep up the necessary pressure to formulate the gas while the other one is manipulating the point.

Take, first a piece of waste wood, and practice several kinds of strokes, until you can regulate the pressure of the point sufficiently to make an even line without dots. Commence the stroke lightly and end it lightly, so there will be no heavy dots at the end of the lines.

The best wood to use is white holly or bass wood for the white wood, or California red wood, when a dark wood is required.

## TOOLS FOR PYROGRAPHY.

FIG. 1 is the pyographic instrument ready for working. B is the bottle that contains the gasoline. D is the bulb which is pressed by the operator's left hand to make the gas. C is the reservoir bulb that holds the air previously to its passing through the rubber tube. F is the rubber tube. A is the cork handle which is held in the operator's right hand. E is the platinum point which should be kept constantly hot. Whenever it goes out heat it again over the alcohol lamp or gas jet.

FIG. 2 shows three different shapes of the platinum point. Shape A is a straight point useful for fine etchings. Shape B has a round blunt point for heavy work. Shape C is the point most commonly used, as it is easily adapted to any style of line or background.

After selecting the wood or article to decorate, draw or trace an appropriate design. Much depends on the design if it is not good no amount of labor can make a satisfactory article and the time is wasted.

Fill the bottle (see B. Fig. 1 )two thirds full of gasoline to which has been added half a teaspoonful of kerosene. Put the cork in firmly. Hold the point in the flame of the alcohol lamp until it is hot, then press the bulb with an even pressure until the point is bright red. It is now ready for use.

Begin to work with a light free stroke. Do not bear heavily on the point. If you wish to burn heavily allow the point to rest quietly until it has burned the required depth. If it is a long line that is to be burned deeply allow the point to move slowly but evenly until the required depth is reached.

## FLEMISH CARVING.

One of the art links that joins the past to the present is "Flemish Carving" or carving in connection with pyrography. The name is taken from some specimens executed by a Flemish artist many years ago in which carving, pyrography and color were combined.

To one not initiated in the mysteries of the art it would be almost impossible to determine how the work was done. But all that one requires is time, patience, and perseverence. With a goodly stock or these an entire house may be most artistically and appropriately decorated.

The carving is roughly done, and therein lies its effectiveness. Hardwood may be used, for there is very little deep burning, the depth being given to the work by the carving tool, the color with the point. Any depth of sepia coloring may be given in this way by using the point lightly. If other colors are required, dyes or acids may be used.

The first directions for this work are similar to those for pyrography as the design is put on the wood in the same manner. Further use of the tools and dyes are given in the part devoted to description of illustrations.

FIG. 24

FIG. 25

FIG. 27

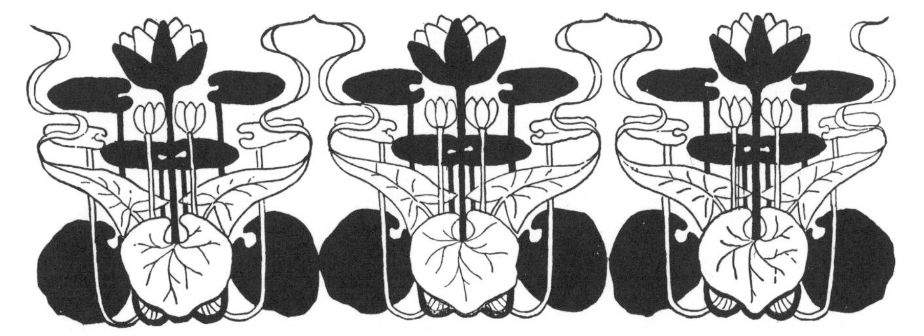

FIG. 26

When a design is to be carved, cut the outline out with the chisel and gouge; using whichever fits the line best. Hold the tool perfectly straight and tap it lightly with the mallet until it cuts into the wood one eighth of an inch. Hold the chisel on an angle and cut the wood from the backgrcund to the depth of first cut. If it is desired to raise the design more than this go around it again in the same manner. When the design is well in relief carve the details of the design until the figures stand out in relief. A rough background is more artistic when pyrography is to be used in connection with carving than a smooth one.

Fig, 3 is the ordinary half inch chisel used in wood carving. It is made of the best steel and will keep a good edge when properly sharpened.

Fig. 4 is the V shaped tool for veining and outlining.

Fig. 5 is the half inch gouge for wood carving. It is used in connection with the chisel to cut out designs and backgrounds.

Fig. 6 is a carving knife that will be found useful in almost every step of the work.

All of these tools must be of the very best steel so that they will hold a good keen edge, otherwise it will be impossible to obtain good results.

⚜

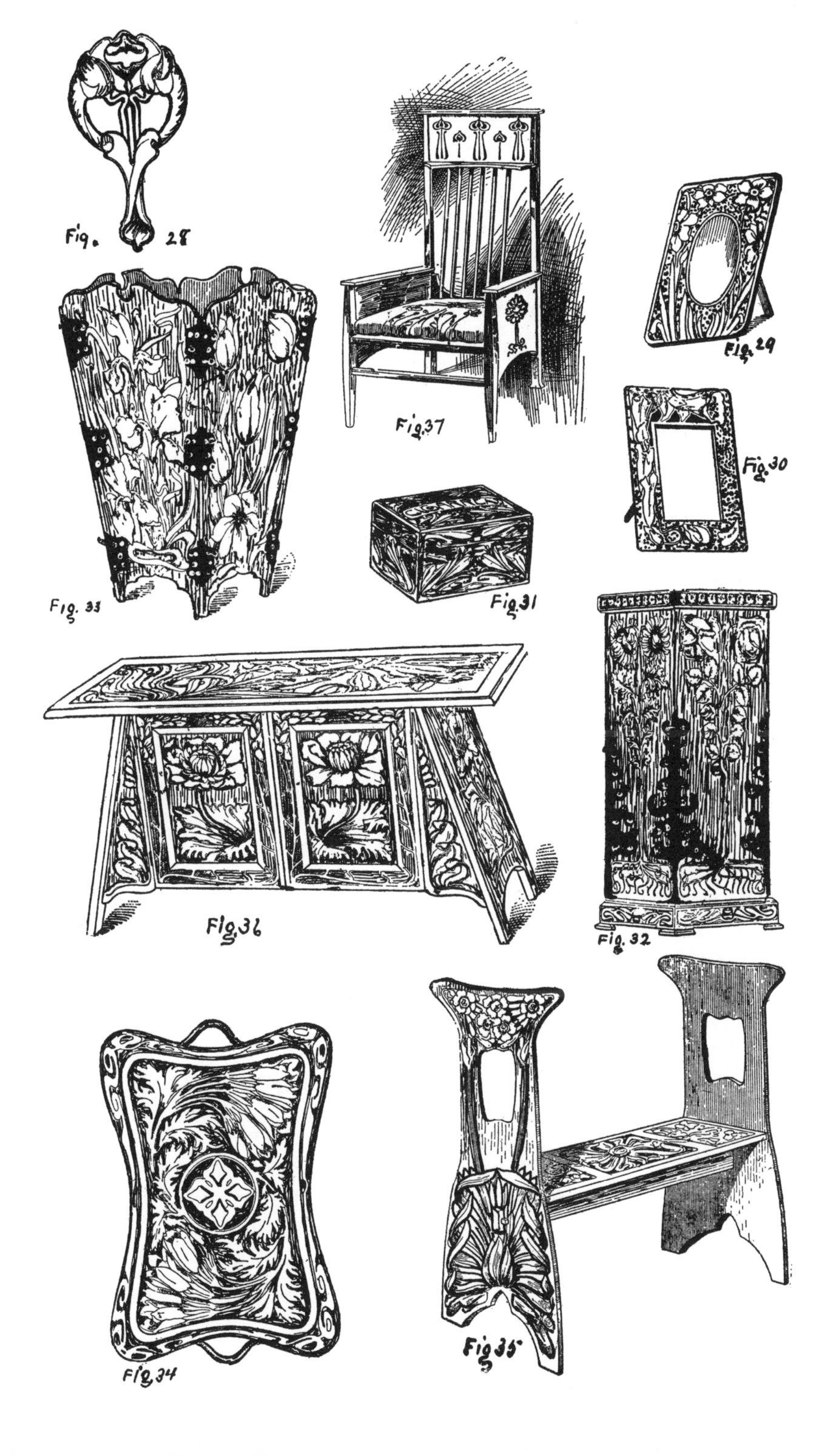
Fig. 28
Fig. 37
Fig. 29
Fig. 30
Fig. 33
Fig. 31
Fig. 36
Fig. 32
Fig. 34
Fig. 35

# DISCRIPTION OF WORKING DESIGNS.

As tne aim of this book is to assist students in learning pyrography and Flemish carving without the aid of a teacher no pains has been spared in the illustrative description. Every article herein described has been made at the Art Craft Institute.

Many of the designs were made by the students.

The object of the school is to teach students "how to do things," and they are expected to design and make a piece of furniture as well as decorate it. But the making and decorating is not all, they must finish it as well. They must know how to use oil, wax or varnish and what the results of each will be. From this veritable workshop we send these few suggestions knowing they will be helpful to advanced teachers as well as beginners.

Fig. 38

FIG. 7 is for a background in pyrography or it may be used for an all over design for boxes etc. First divide the surface to be decorated into half inch squares with a pencil, then draw the cross lines with the hot point as shown in the illustration.

FIGS. 8, 9 and 10 illustrate four methods of decorating backgrounds.

The space to be decorated is first divided evenly into half inch squares and burned. In FIG. 8 place the hot point exactly in the center of the square then burn around it, an irregular square, as illustrated.

FIG, 9 shows two different treatments of the daisy square. In the first the daisy is burned dark with a light background. In the second the daisy is outlined leaving the center light with a dark background. In FIG. 10 the daisy is light and the background is filled in with soft lines.

FIG. 11 is a background made by holding the point in different positions and burning with short broad strokes until the surface is covered with an even tone of brown.

FIG. 12 With a ruler and pencil divide the surface to be decorated into one half inch squares. Place the point at the intersection of the pencil lines and make a short quick stroke heavier near the center than at the end. Make four of these heavy strokes as illustrated, then fill in between with delicate lines. This is also a good suggestion for an all over design. The squares may be one inch or more in size if desired.

FIG. 13 is similar to Fig, 12 except that the design has eight petals.

Fig. 39
Fig. 40
Fig. 41
Fig. 42
Fig. 44
Fig. 43

Fig. 14 is made by first dividing the squares diagonally and burning the lines. At the intersection of the crossed lines burn the decoration as illustrated.

Fig. 15 is a series of short lines placed so close together that they will cover a large surface with an even tone of brown.

Fig. 16 is the fish bone background. It can be used diagonally or perpendicular.

Fig. 17 is composed of irregular cherry blossoms so near together that they form a perfect background.

Figs. 18, 19, 20, 21 and 23 illustrate the variety that may be given to back grounds by different groupings of the lines.

Fig. 22 is the wave background, especially useful in designs when it is desirable to illustrate decorative water effects.

Figs. 24, 25, 26 and 27 are designs for borders, that may be used for frames, tables, chests chairs or in almost any place where a border is necessary.

Fig. 28 In this design for a hand glass pyrography and carving are united. After the design is drawn upon the wood, the wood is fastened to the table with a clamp to hold it firm. The edge is then rounded off at the sides with the chisel. The design is carved in low relief according to illustration. As soon as the carving is finished the deepest parts are burned vcry dark and gradually shaded out to light. As this mirror was made of three ply bass wood the entire edge was burned very dark.

Fig. 45
Fig. 46
Fig. 47
Fig. 48
Fig. 49
Fig. 50
Fig. 51
Fig. 52
Fig. 53.b.
Fig. 53

FIGS. 29 and 30 are picture frames in pyrography. The shading of the flowers and leaves are all done with the point. When the burning is completed the flowers in fig. 29 should be stained yellow with gamboge and the leaves green with a wash made of Hookers green and gamboge. The frame (fig. 30 ) is in the natural color of the wood, as the design is not adapted to color effects. Color should not be used unless it enhances the best features of the design.

FIG. 31 is a cigar box decorated with pyrography. The background is burned very dark and deep. The conventionalized lily which forms the decoration is carefully shaded with the point. Inside of cover is decorated with Fig. 43.

FIG. 32 The original design of this umbrella stand is 10 x 24 inches The design is first roughly carved, making the flowers quite prominent while the stems and leaves gradually fade away into the roughly carved back ground. The petals of the flowers, the leaves and conventional borders are lightly touched with copper dye (this dye is prepared expressly for the school work.) The copper plates which hold the corners firmly in place were made for this piece and follow the idea of the original design. Small copper plates are placed at the top of each of the corners and the whole completes a most artistic umbrella stand.

FIG. 33 The same idea is carried out in the waste paper basket as in the umbrella stand, except the copper plates that hold it together are in the form of hinges left plain and fastened on with fancy copper nails.

Fig. 54 Fig. 55

Fig. 56

Fig. 57

FIG. 34 This large wooden tray is decidedly unique in style and finish. We do not forget that it is to be used for a tray and therefore must have a comparatively smoth surface so that things will sit on it securely. Always remember this in the decoration of table tops, chair seats and all similar articles. The outline is lightly burned. The flowers and leaves carefully shaded with the point. Tint the the flowers and leaves with antique green, deep yellow and orange with here and there a touch of deep rich red, (for this purpose it is best to use the prepared stains.) The result is a tray that looks as if it might be a treasured heirloom.

FIG. 35. This beautiful window seat was made for a special window. The ends are 40 inches high. The seat 20 inches wide by 40 inches long. It is made of one inch poplar. The ends and seat are carved and decorated before it is put together. The color is what is known as weathered oak, with the slightest touch of orange and red in the flowers, and green in the leaves. The whole effect being gray with just a glimmer of color.

FIG. 36. This combination seat and linen chest is one of the most beautiful pieces of its kind, and can, like the others, be easily made to fit any place. We are fast learning that furniture is best adapted to its purpose and place when it is designed expressly for that purpose and place. The seat is 18 inches high the top 20 x 48 inches. It is fitted with shelves underneath. The doors are hinged. The wood used here is the Califormia red wood one inch in thickness. The design is first carved in bold relief,

Fig 58
Fig.62
Fig.59
Fig.60
Fig 63
Fig.61

then shaded with the point. No stain or color of any kind is used as the natural color of the wood is exquisite when simply finished with wax, using no varnish.

FIG. 37 is a chair made of solid oak stained black. The design which is thoroughly dignified and true to its position is burned in. No color what ever is used. The cushion is of dark green leather decorated with pyrography. This chair is plain dignified and artistic.

FIG. 38 As we said in the beginning pyrography is just as suitable a decoration for leather as for wood. The Japanese girl watering her flowets was used to decorate the leather cover of a portfolio which was made to hold some Japanese pictures. The original design is 6 x 10 inches but it can be furnished in a larger size if desired.

FIG. 39 It is frequently a question as to the best means of finishing the inside of glove, handkerchief and other box covers, and we have found nothing more satisfactory than a carefully etched landscape. Fig. 39 was used to decorate the inside cover of a large shirt waist box. Figs. 41, 42 and 43 are admirable for glove, handkerchief and jewel box covers.

FIG. 40 makes a perfect decoration for the ends of a folding bookrack.

FIG. 44 is one of three panels used in the decoration of a dining room. This sketch is from Winslow Homers painting the "Farmer Boy" and is admirably adapted to the purpose. The work is in pyrography without carving or color.

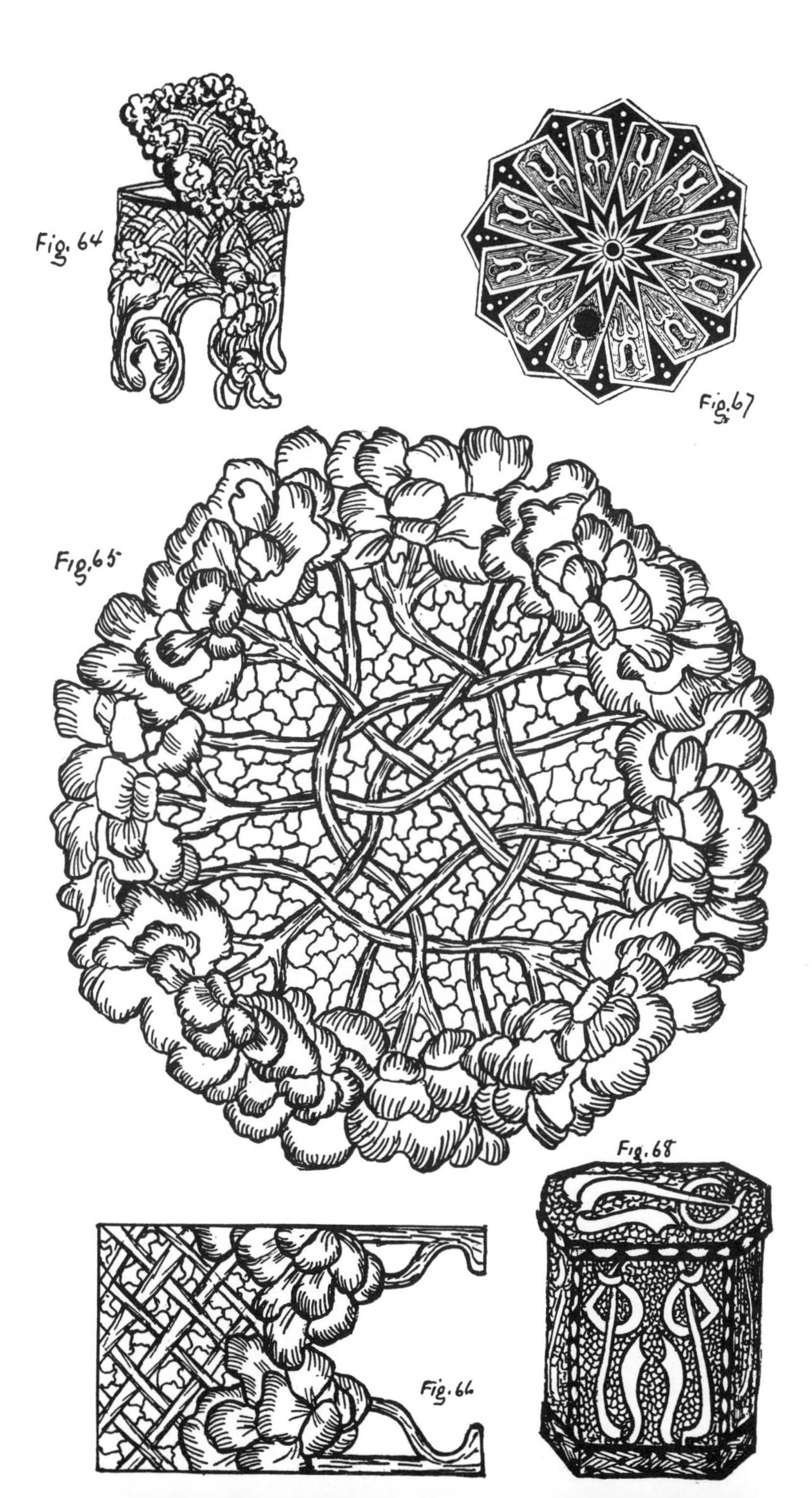
Fig. 64
Fig. 67
Fig. 65
Fig. 68
Fig. 66

FIG. 45 represents a portfolio covered with dark brown leather, having straps of the same. The inside leaves are of heavy brown paper for photographs they are fastened to the cover with the same straps that decorate the outside. The holes through which the straps pass are burned through both leather and paper with the point. After the straps are passed through the holes they are fastened to the outside of the cover with glue or paste. The word "Photographs" in decorative letters is burned lightly accross the outside of the cover. In burning leather care must be taken not to burn holes through the skin.

FIG. 46. This beautiful screen has a plain frame of basswood, etchedwith a pyrographic design. Light brown velveteen is used for the panels. The design of Iris is first burned on the velvet. The petals of the flowers and buds are cut out of leather and glued in place. While they are still wet, the edges are pressed down tightly into the pile of the velvet, this raises the flowers somewhat. The velvet must be stretched tightly on a board or table before the work is commenced. As soon as the glue is dry burn the veins of the petals, and shade them with the point. This screen is beautiful when the work is carefully executed.

FIG. 47 is one, of a row of butterflies, that was used for a border for a table. Place the butterflies so the tips of the wings will just touch, then burn as illustrated.

FIGS. 48, 49, 50 and 51 The original of these monograms are four inches high. Monograms are almost always appropriate for decorations and may be used upon almost any kind of material,

Fig 69

Fig. 71
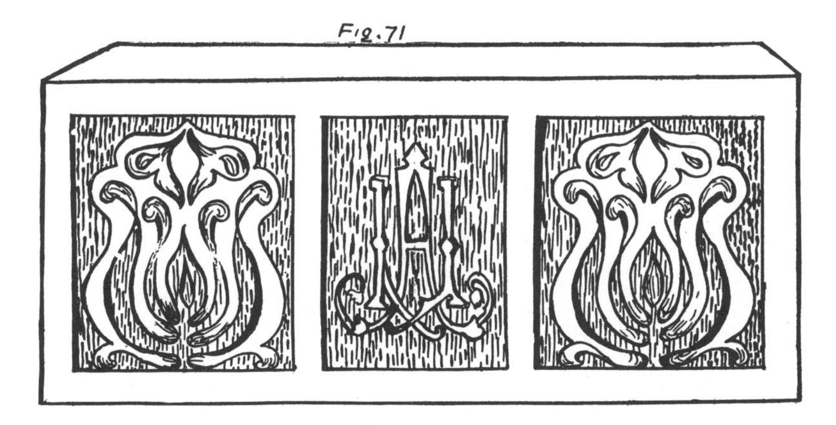

Fig. 72

Fig 70

FIG. 52 is a suitable decoration for a key rack. Size of the original design is 6x8 inches.

FIG. 53 was originally designed for the back of a settle 32x48 inches, but it can be reduced to any size and used for other things as well. The open space in the center may be filled with a quotation if desired or it may be left plain as illustrated. The design is for pyrography only, no carving or color being used.

FIG. 53b is a border design illustrating chinese pennies. It may be continued indefinitely by repetition and is remarkably decorative for a great variety of purposes.

FIG. 54 When a student has had sufficient practice to feel confidence in handling the carving tools and point there is nothing that appeals more to the artistic temperment than the making of special pieces of furniture. The Greek chair herein illustrated can be easily made at home. The wood is oak, but any other material may be used. The end pieces are 36 inches high. The seat is 20 inches wide by 36 long. The end panels are divided into 4 inch circles, and in each of the circles the design of fir cones (see Fig. 55)is broadly carved. When the carving is finished, the needles are burned in very dark and deep near the cones growing lighter as they near the ends. The stem follows the circle somewhat irregularly and forms a frame for each group of cones. The ends of the posts are finished with a carved cone at the top touched in the shadows with the hot point. The seat is carved and burned to match the ends, If oak is the material used for this chair it should be stained a dull green and finished with wax.

Fig.73
Fig 74
Fig.75
Fig.76
Fig.77
Fig.78
Fig 79
Fig. 80

Fig. 56 The Japanese dragon in this illustration forms the only decoration on the front of a ladies writing desk. It is burned in and has no color except a suspicion of dull red about the mouth. The rest of the wood work is plain with a weathered oak finish.

Fig. 57 is a suitable design for the center of a box cover, The original was designed for an oblong table top done in pyrography.

Fig. 58 shows half of a picture frame in pyrography.

Figs. 59 and 60 are Greek borders tnat may be used to fine advantage in pyrography as the uneven line made with the point gives them a most artistic effect.

Fig. 61 is a border for a book cover to be made of leather and decorated with pyrography.

Figs. 62 and 63 are Japanese designs that may be used most effectively for decorative panels in pyrography. The original designs are 12x16 inches. They were used as decorations for the doors of a specimen cabinet.

Fig. 64 illustrates a tabourette in which the design is first boldly carved, then burned. The conventional flowers and leaves are tinted dull red and green with suggestions of blue. The shape of the tabourette is formed by the design.

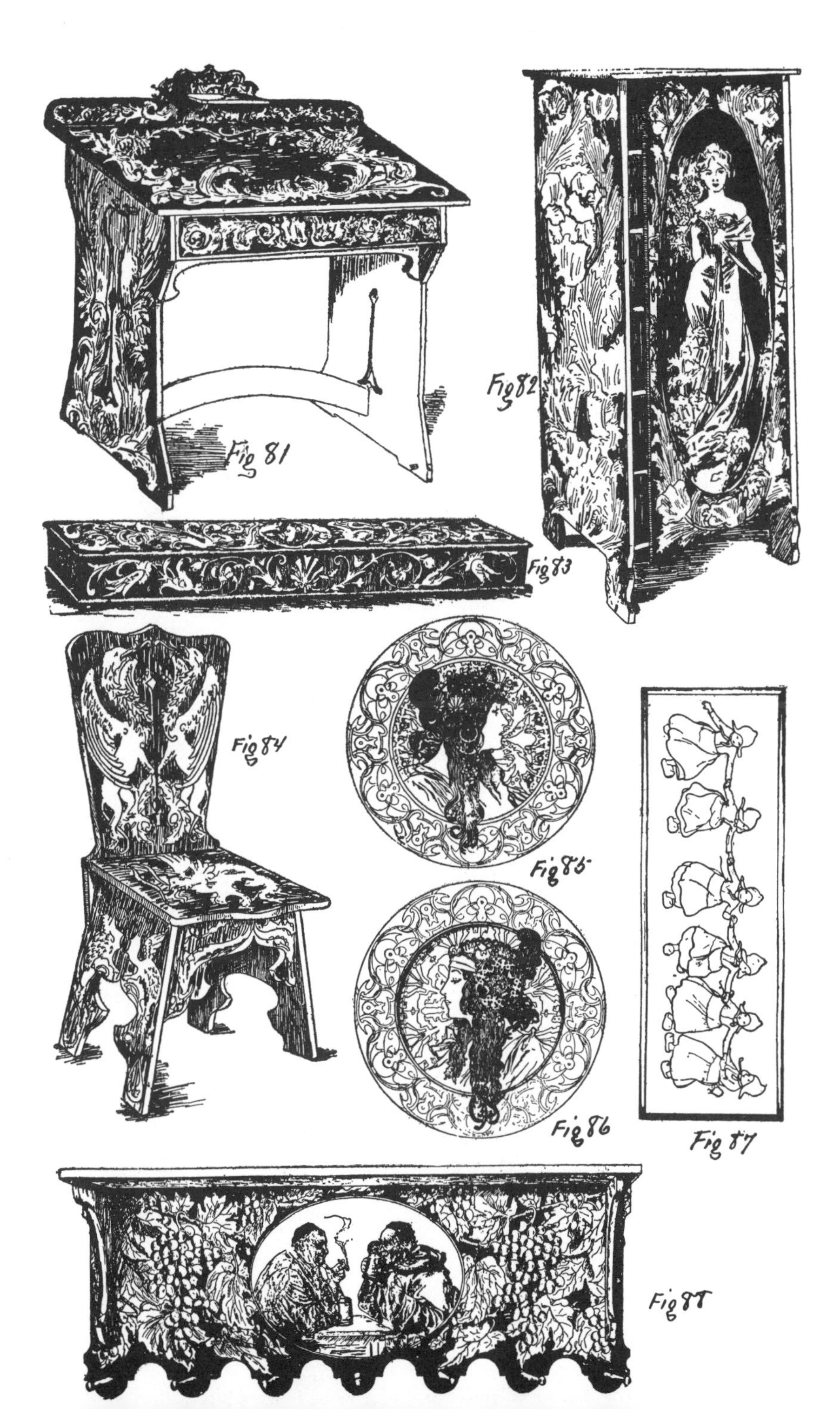

Fig 81

Fig 82

Fig 83

Fig 84

Fig 85

Fig 86

Fig 87

Fig 88

FIG. 65 is a table top carved and burned the same as FIG. 64. It is 24 inches accross the top. There are eight legs (see Fig. 66) 26 inches high. There is no carving on this table except in the border which is done in low relief, all the rest of the design is worked in pyrography. The table is of California red wood in its natural color, finished with lacco and wax.

FIG. 67 is designed for a table top 20 x 20 inches. It has, when finished, the appearance of inlaid work. The plain black parts of the design are stained black. The star in the center is dark red and green. The conventional flowers are red and green. The space around them is light blue, and the flat bands are red. First outline the design with the point in even lines. Fill in between the lines with the color as directed, when dry finish with three coats of lacco. As soon as one coat is dry put on another. Let the lacco dry for twenty four hours, rub it down with pumice stone and water until it is perfectly smooth, then finish with wax.

FIG. 68 is a hat box 18 inches high by 18 inches wide. The cover is hinged. The inside is lined with old gold satin. The design is in pyrography, stained a copper color. The flat moulding around the bottom is nailed on with copper headed tacks.

FIGS. 69, 70, 71 and 72 are designs for linen chests. Each is 48 inches long by 20 wide and 18 high. The designs are carved and burned, then stained with dull reds, greens and blues until they take on an antique appearance. Fig. 70 shows the design for cover of Fig. 69, and Fig. 72 shows cover of Fig. 71. Both chests are made of oak, but as that makes them very heavy, many prefer the lighter basswood.

FIGS. 73, 74, 75, 76, 77, 78, 79 and 80 are especially designed for sofa pillows. The orginal designs are twenty inches square. The outline is in pyrography on different colored leathers. Figs. 73 and 75 are on green ooze leather. Fig. 74 is burned on red leather. Fig. 76 is on white sheepskin and the design is stained with tapestry dyes. Fig. 77 is on light green leather, with the leaves stained a dark green. Fig. 78 is gorgeous in Egyptian colorings on yellow leather. Fig. 79 is a Golf cover having a colored flag. Fig, 80 is a Japanese doll wearing a yellow dress decorated with black figures. Fig. 76 may be cut out after it is burned. The edge of the design scorched, then pasted firmly on a red or green leather. This allows the under color to show through the desig n.

FIG. 81. This writing desk is one of the conveniences of the modern home. It may be purchased ready made in basswood or any carpenter can make one. The design should be first burned in good strong outline, then shaded with the point. The color used is old blue, green and red. Fig. 84 is a chair that goes with the desk and is treated to correspond.

FIG. 82 illustrates a most covenient and practical music cabinet. As it is used in connection with the piano it should be finished to correspond with that instrument after the design has been burned in.

FIG. 83. This dresser case is made nearly as long as the dresser upon which it is placed. The inside is divided into compartments for handkerchief, gloves, jewelry etc. The design is burned deeply and colored to suit the taste, then finished with lacco and wax as before described.

FIGS. 85 anb 86 are decorative plaques designed by Mucha. After the design is burned in, the heads are colored to give them an oriental effect.

FIG. 87. Illustrates a row of those famous Dutch babies. This design is especially adapted to the decoration of children's rooms and furniture.

FIG. 88. In this day and age of the world when everyone is collecting steins no home would be complete without at least one stein rack. The one illustrated is well designed. The center panel is taken from a well known Dutch painting, and the grape border is quite appropriate for the subject. Carve the grapes and leaves in low relief,then finish with the point. Color the grapes and leaves with purples, reds, yellows and greens. Burn the center panel and leave it in the natural coloring of the wood. Finish with lacco and wax in the usual manner.